# *Elements of*

◆

# *I*NFORMATION

# *S*YSTEMS

◆

# *Components and Architecture*

◆

## LEVENT V. ORMAN

**Cornell University**

MACMILLAN PUBLISHING COMPANY • NEW YORK
COLLIER MACMILLAN CANADA, INC. • TORONTO
MAXWELL MACMILLAN INTERNATIONAL PUBLISHING GROUP
NEW YORK • OXFORD • SINGAPORE • SYDNEY

Editor: Charles Stewart, Jr.
Production Supervisor: Kathryn Cianci
Production Manager: Pamela Kennedy Oborski
Designer: Patrice Fodero
Illustrations: G&H Soho
This book was set in 11/13 Aster by Waldman Graphics, Inc. printed and bound by Arcata Graphics/Halliday.
The cover was printed by Lehigh Press.

Copyright © 1991 by Macmillan Publishing Company, a division of Macmillan, Inc.

Printed in the United States of America

Macmillan Publishing Company
866 Third Avenue, New York, New York 10022

Collier Macmillan Canada, Inc.

**LIBRARY OF CONGRESS CATALOGING-IN-PUBLICATION DATA**

Orman, Levent V.
   Elements in information systems : components and architecture / Levent V. Orman.
      p.   cm.
   ISBN 0-02-389475-X
   1. Electronic data processing.   2. Computer architecture.
3. System design.   I. Title.
QA76.075   1991
004.2′2—dc20                                              89-13636
                                                              CIP

Printing: 1 2 3 4 5 6 7 8 9     Year: 1 2 3 4 5 6 7 8 9 0

♦

# Preface

This book is about the elements of an information system. It studies the components comprising an information system, their structure, their organization, their design, maintenance, and implementation, and their relationships to each other. It is not about the hardware required to build an information system, and it is not about the interaction between the information system and the organization that utilizes it. A variety of issues ranging from the acquisition and evaluation of hardware to impact on the organization, from success factors in building information systems to personnel requirements of an information systems department, from the economics of information production to the human perception and utilization of information are left to more advanced courses. This book concentrates on the system itself, and mostly its architecture. It is suggested as a first course in information systems for undergraduates or professional students, immediately following an "Introduction to Computers and Computer Programming" course. For professional students who have never been exposed to computer programming, a one-week intensive seminar on

BASIC or PASCAL programming should be sufficient as a pre-requisite. Each chapter lists possible student projects at the end. Computer projects are recommended for students who have access to commercial software, since hands-on experience is valuable on many of these topics. The text can be used as a two-semester introduction with extensive use of projects and commercial software, or as a one-semester course with limited use of hands-on projects.

The pedagogical principle underlying the book is teaching by example. Progressively more difficult examples are used to introduce progressively more difficult concepts, with no formal treatment. Stylized notations are developed to demonstrate linguistic concepts without a detailed syntax. This approach appears to provide the intuition and insight most appropriate for professional students and undergraduates. However, learning by doing also has disadvantages. It requires the students to get involved at a more detailed level than with discussion type courses, and to get their hands dirty. Nevertheless, the time investment required by this approach is often worthwhile both because of the concrete insight gained and because of the permanence of the knowledge acquired.

The course is critical for those planning careers in information systems, and for those planning to be managers, or other professional users of information systems. Both the designers and the users of information systems need to know the technical and the political issues surrounding systems development. Research and past experience clearly shows that those information systems built without direct participation of the end users are highly likely to fail. In particular, end users have to understand the technical alternatives, ranging from highly flexible systems that can adapt to changing information needs quickly and efficiently but require large initial capital expenditures, to rigid and inflexible systems that can provide only explicitly planned and specified information but inexpensively, and a variety of options in between. The users have to appreciate the political process involved in building a shared system where not all needs and requirements can be met equally successfully, and compromises are often necessary, and the nature of compromises is technically complex. Probably more than any other large capital investment, the design of information systems requires an extensive participation by management and a deep understanding and appreciation of technology, because of the intimate relationship between managers and their information systems, and their total dependence on formal information for their daily activities. A second reason why managers have to understand and appreciate information systems is the effect these systems have on managerial jobs. Information systems are changing the nature of managerial activity, by supporting it in novel ways, by simplifying it, and sometimes by taking over entire tasks. Consequently, managers find themselves either in need of sophisticated systems support to remain competitive, or in actual competition with automated systems. Either way, management indifference to or ignorance of systems concepts is not wise in a modern organization, no matter how painfully technical those concepts may be.

Levent V. Orman

◆

# Acknowledgments

I would like to thank the faculty and staff at Cornell University Johnson Graduate School of Management for the intellectual environment, my colleagues Richard Conway and Akhil Kumar for valuable discussions, Professors Edward Stohr and Mohan Tanniru for detailed comments, Database and Systems Analysis students for careful reviewing of the manuscript, Computing Services staff for excellent computing support, Macmillan editorial staff for valuable advice, Valorie Adams and Tina Weyland for expert typing, WSH music room for a warm environment in which to write, Constance Ziemian for a thoughtful instructor's manual, and Kathy Byun for proofreading and emotional support.

◆

# Contents

## *Part III. Knowledge Base Application Systems*   185

# Chapter 1

◆

# Information Systems

An *information system* is a system that collects, stores, retrieves, processes, and displays information. There is a myth that associates information systems solely with computers. In fact, many information systems commonly used in our daily lives do not involve computers. Some primitive examples of noncomputerized information systems are phone books, dictionaries, file cabinets, library card catalogs, and even libraries themselves. At the other extreme, some of the most sophisticated information systems do not involve computers either. Most managerial activity can be characterized as information processing and the managers can be viewed as information systems. In fact, most human organization and social institutions can be characterized as information systems and this mechanical view constitutes a major school of thought in Organization Theory. However, this book will concentrate on computerized information systems.

The definition of an information system as a system that operates on information begs the definitions of "system" and "information." A *system* is a purposeful collection of interrelated components. An information system is certainly a system, and identifying and studying its components and their interrelationships is the subject of this book. *Information*, on the other hand, is an elusive concept, and it is difficult to define.

Like all difficult concepts in science, the common approach to understand it is to identify its components and their relationships. Information has two formal components, in addition to some informal and poorly understood components. The two formal components are *data* and *procedures*.

## Data

A *data item* consists of three components: an *entity* about which information is being collected, an *attribute* that describes the nature of the information being collected, and a *value* attached to that attribute.

◆ **EXAMPLE 1.1.** ◆

"Smith's age is 25" is a data item where Smith is the entity, age is the attribute, and 25 is the value.

The entities are outside the system. They are things of interest to the users of the information system. They should not be confused with the names of entities stored as identifiers within the system. The real-life person Smith should be clearly distinguished from the character string "SMITH" used to identify him within the system. The character string "SMITH" is merely a value of the attribute NAME of an entity. It is important to remember that a data item is a triplet of entity-attribute-value, and values themselves without description do not constitute data items. All data are collections of these data item triplets.

A *database* is a collection of interrelated data. Consequently, it contains entities, attributes, values, and also relationships among data items. *Database management* is the art and science of managing databases, and a *database management system* is a software product that aids in that task. Database management activities include maintaining and updating the database, insuring its integrity and security, keeping it functioning properly and efficiently, and maximizing its availability to its authorized users through appropriate languages and access methods. A database management system automates some of these functions, leaving others to human *system analysts,* all under the supervision of a *database manager.*

## Procedures

*Procedures* are transformations of data. A procedure can be viewed as a black box that receives some data (input), and transforms it and delivers other data (output).

◆ **EXAMPLE 1.2.** ◆

"Smith's salary increases 10 percent every year" is a procedure that transforms the salary value for Smith.

The characterization of the nature of a transformation is called the *procedure definition.* All general-purpose programming languages provide facilities for procedure definition. Procedures can be expressed by sequential instructions to a central processor of a computer to modify stored values in a main memory. For completeness, in addition to sequential instructions, loop and conditional instructions are also required. *Looping* involves repetition of an instruction until a given condition holds, and *conditional instructions* involve executing an instruction only if a given condition holds. Procedures can also be expressed only in terms of simple conditionals with no looping and sequential instructions, as we will see in Part III.

## *Types of Information Systems*

Three types of information systems are characterized by the extent to which they facilitate sharing of information. *Data processing systems* provide for minimal sharing. They involve stand-alone independent systems custom-developed for each application. *Database application systems* are characterized by organization-wide sharing of data. Sharing has definite advantages such as reduced redundancy, but the users have to learn how to locate and retrieve their information from a central utility, and the central utility has to be managed professionally to accommodate a variety of users and applications efficiently. Finally, *knowledge base application systems* are characterized by the sharing of procedures and a central utility to manage procedures. The advantage of nonredundancy, and the disadvantage of using and maintaining a central utility, are even more pronounced in knowledge base application systems. This book is organized around this classification, with three parts, each corresponding to a type of information system.

Data processing systems are the earliest examples of computerized information systems. They are application-specific, and provide minimal description of ther contents. Typical examples are payroll, billing, and inventory control systems. Since each system is dedicated to a particular application, the description is geared toward the specialist in that application, and it is not very extensive. It is usually provided in the form of printed manuals of procedures and standards, and the users are expected to have considerable insight into both the application and the inner workings of the system that serves the application. Sharing among these systems is minimal. Part I of this book is about data processing systems.

Database application systems capitalize on the advantages of sharing data. They are commonly used to build *managment information systems* since it is easily observed that many applications within an organization use the same operational data for reporting purposes, and the duplication of effort to collect, store, and retrieve those data is significant in data processing systems. As the number of applications increases, to serve all levels of management by reprocessing the same operational data, the amount of duplication also increases and quickly becomes intolerable. Moreover, such duplication is often less than perfect, leading to interapplication inconsistencies. A single, centrally controlled database shared by all applications of an organization is an effective solution to this problem utilized by Database Application Systems. The major concern with such large shared databases is the difficulty of describing data objectively, independent of individual applications, to facilitate use by a multitude of diverse applications. Data models and data dictionaries are used extensively to describe data; and *data semantics*, the study of the meaning of data independent of the individual applications that use them, is a field of study critical to database application systems. Part II of this book deals with Database Application Systems.

Knowledge base application systems capitalize on the advantages of sharing procedures. They are commonly used to build decision support systems, since it is easily observed that many applications designed to support strategic decisions involve similar procedures, with minor differences introduced in personalizing these applications to aid a particular user. The duplication of effort to design, implement, and test these procedures is significant in data processing and database application systems. As the number of applications increases, to provide the personalized on-line support these systems envision, the amount of procedural duplication also increases and quickly becomes intolerable, since the personalized on-line support requires many personalized versions of the same basic application, and each version has to be modified many times in its lifetime to keep abreast with the changes in its user's abilities, attitudes, knowledge, and beliefs. Moreover, the duplication is often less than perfect, leading to interapplication inconsistencies and less than efficient procedures. A single centrally controlled knowledge base shared by all applications is an effective solution to this problem utilized by knowledge base application systems. The major concern with the large

shared knowledge bases is the difficulty of describing procedures objectively, independent of individual applications, to
facilitate use by a multitude of diverse applications. Procedural
models, rules, functions, objects, and frames are some of the
tools used in describing procedures by knowledge base application systems. Part III of this book introduces knowledge base
application systems.

## Agents and Tools

There are four agents in the environment of an information
system. These agents have distinct responsibilities and they
have to cooperate and communicate effectively to create a successful system environment. These four agents are

1. End users
2. Analysts/Designers
3. Implementors
4. System

The *end users* are the beneficiaries of the system. They receive informaton from the system to fulfill their responsibilities
in other areas. They are a diverse group, but they are characterized by job responsibilities in specialties other than information systems, and limited expertise and commitment in
systems issues. The end users are expected to have some involvement in systems issues to insure that their needs are met
correctly and effectively, but their involvement is limited due
to their other responsibilities. The *system*, on the other hand,
usually refers to all the automated components and their administrators. *Analyst/designers* and *implementors* are interme-
diaries that link the end users to the system. These interme-
diaries are necessary since the systems are technically complex
and the end users have neither the background nor the time to
master all the complexities and technical details. Intermedi-

aries are expected to facilitate communication between the end users and systems. Analysts/Designers tend to be more user-oriented with more of a business background, while implementors tend to be more system-oriented with a more technical background. The analysts and designers tend to use the same tools and often are the same personnel. *Analysis* refers to the study of an existing system and *design* refers to the creation of a new system. Studying the old system, its strengths and shortcomings is often closely coupled with the creation of a new system or modification of the old, and hence these two activities are often indistinguishable. The communication is hierarchical from end users down the line to the systems, and from the systems back up the line to the end users. There are three stages of communication among the four agents and each stage has its unique set of tools and devices for data processing, database application, and knowledge base application systems. The four agents, the three stages of communication among them, and the tools they use are shown in Figure 1.1.

In a data processing environment, the four agents are most distinct, and the communication stages are clearly defined. In addition to data flow diagrams and system specification tech-

| Agent | | Tools | | |
|---|---|---|---|---|
| | | DP | DBA | KBA |
| End User | | | | |
| | Stage I | English<br>Data flow diagrams<br>System specification<br>    techniques | External data models<br>User oriented languages | Rules<br>Specification<br>    languages |
| Analyst/Designer | | | | |
| | Stage II | Procedure descriptions<br>File descriptions | Data models<br>Database languages<br>Report writers | |
| Implementor | | | | |
| | Stage III | Programming languages<br>Physical data structures | | |
| System | | | | |

Figure 1.1. Agents, communication stages, and the tools used by Data Processing, Database Application, and Knowledge Base Application Systems.

niques, natural languages, informal interviews, and detailed manuals are used extensively in user-analyst communication. Analysts in turn provide more formal descriptions of both procedures and files to implementors who develop the computer programs and physical data structures. In a database application environment, sharing of data requires general implementation of data, independent of individual applications, greatly reducing the implementor's job, since shared data have to be implemented only once for the whole organization, not for each application. Reduction in the implementor's responsibilities allows other agents such as analysts and systems to expand into that territory and eliminate implementor positions. This environment is dominated by database management systems. End users deal with external data models and user-oriented languages. Analysts are concerned with data models and database languages. High-level languages such as report writers or extended database languages allow analysts to bypass implementors and interact directly with the system. In a knowledge base application environment, sharing of procedures requires general implementation of procedures and control. Systems are built from bits and pieces of information with no overall analysis or design, thus reducing the responsibilities of analysts. Reducing the responsibilities of analysts allows other agents such as end users and the system to expand into that territory and eliminate some analyst positions. This environment is dominated by end user languages, specification languages, and rule-based systems where end users interact with the system directly in developing and using their applications.

## Commercial Examples

Three generations of information systems are characterized by the degree of sharing they facilitate. A good analogy exists between information and food as consumer goods. Both goods have to be gathered, stored, and processed before consumption. A data processing system is similar to a farmers' market, where the consumer has to contact many farmers for his raw materials since each farmer produces a specific crop, and it is the consumer's responsibility to gather all of his ingredients from appropriate sources. The task is time consuming and laborious and usually requires a homemaker's full-time attention. Similarly, the user in a data processing environment is responsible for putting together all of his data and processing it. This task is also time consuming and often technical, and most users find it necessary to hire a specialist for the job (a programmer, and often a whole data processing department). A database environment is analogous to a supermarket, where a centrally controlled shared structure contains all raw materials needed for all consumers in a particular location. The immediate task is to organize a large number of items so that they can be easily located, and to provide tools to consumers to locate and retrieve the items they need efficiently. Similarly, the user in a database environment gets all of his data from a large shared structure. The structure is managed professionally to organize large amounts of data so that all users can efficiently find and retrieve their data. Users are given elaborate tools such as data languages to retrieve their own data. A knowledge base environment is analogous to a restaurant, where a large shared structure not only contains all the raw materials but also all the processing talent and tools, and a consumer only needs to learn how to use such a structure to put together a variety of raw materials and processing methods to produce a consumable good that fits his needs and tastes. Similarly, the user in a knowledge base environment gets all of his data and his procedures from a large shared structure. The user has to learn to use such a complex shared structure, but once he acquires the skill he can put together many shared components of data and procedures to produce his own information, eliminating most of the need for a private structure and specialized employees.

Many commercial examples of all three types of information systems are available:

## Accounting

The earliest examples of data processing systems involve the automation of bookkeeping. Accounts payable and accounts receivable were captured in files, and simple programs that update the files. T accounts, ledgers, and master accounts quickly became obsolete and were replaced by master and transaction files, update programs, and sort/merge procedures. In the database environment, financial and cost data, in addition to production, marketing and external data are all combined into a central reservoir. All management reporting needs are satisfied from this single shared source, eliminating redundancy, inconsistency, and inaccessibility, leading to management information systems. In the knowledge base environment, many standard accounting procedures are incorporated into the shared system. Consequently, managers can receive not only accounting reports, but also personalized advice on policy issues such as tax management, depreciation of capital assets, and buy or lease decisions, leading to decision support systems.

## Banking

Data processing systems revolutionized consumer banking with automatic teller machines (ATM) and magnetic strip cards, eliminating many jobs both in the front and in the back office. By lowering the transaction costs, they facilitated the creation of many new financial instruments such as negotiable orders of withdrawal (NOW) accounts, cash management accounts (CMA), and money market accounts, which all allowed in one way or another for small funds to be invested for short periods. By changing the economies of scale, they created a move from small local banks to giant national and global banking institutions. Many government regulations protecting small local banks and thrifts were lobbied against heavily and were either relaxed or totally abandoned. The McFadden Act of 1927, the Glass-Steagall Act of 1933, and Regulation Q of the Federal Reserve are some examples. Transaction processing systems require huge initial investments, but cut down unit transaction costs up to 50 percent. Moreover, the transaction costs remain low until almost the system capacity is reached. This environment results in large economies of scale, so much so that Shearson-Loeb-Rhoades, one of the largest securities firms in the United States, acquired Lehman Brothers-Kuhn-Loeb, a blue chip investment banking firm, in 1984 without any additional transaction costs in its back office. This and other mergers created the Shearson-Lehman-American Express financial empire. The economies of scale in transaction processing also created companies whose sole business is pooling and processing the transactions of other companies. The Savings Bank Trust Company of Woodmere, New York is such an example. It is owned and operated by 97 savings and loan institutions throughout New York, and its sole function is to provide transaction processing to its banks. It supports automated teller machines as well as human tellers through a computer network and on-line transaction processing. It also acts as a clearinghouse for all checks written against its member banks. The database environment provided large shared financial databanks containing credit information. Many new companies sprang up to collect credit information about individuals and corporations from many sources and make these large financial databanks available to bank loan officers to determine the credit-worthiness of loan applicants. These large shared structures grew to national proportions. Dun & Bradstreet is a prime example of such an information service conglomerate, which made $425 million in 1985 from its domestic credit information services alone. In the knowledge base environment, many rules and procedures used in processing loan applications are incorporated into the system. Consequently, the system not only retrieves credit information about a customer and funds availability information about the bank, but also gives advice on the approval and the desirability of a loan. It provides a risk analysis that is tailored for the needs and preferences of each loan officer although the information comes from a shared resource. American International Group Company is a leader in this area with a number of internally developed systems for risk analysis to assist commercial lending.

## Securities Exchange

Securities exchange is a heavily transaction-oriented market. Large numbers of shares change hands every minute and the transactions have to be processed swiftly to insure that prices accurately reflect the market conditions. An obvious candidate for data processing systems, the securities industry has been slow in automation due to intense regulation and the conservative nature of the industry. Nevertheless, many data processing systems have been built both in the United States and abroad to automate the clearing of transactions. National Association of Securities Dealers Automated Quotations (NASDAQ) in the United States, Computer Assisted Trading System (CATS) in Canada, and Stock Exchange Automated Quotations (SEAQ) in England managed to almost completely automate exchanges and eliminate the need for trading floors, market specialists, and even some brokers. Many other more limited systems have been designed and installed. Open Automatic Reporting System (OARS) is used by the New York Stock Exchange to execute small orders entered before the market opened. Designated Order Turnaround System (DOT) is also used by the New York Stock Exchange to transmit orders of unlisted stocks from member firms directly to floor specialists. Intermarket Trading System (ITS) is used to interconnect the New York, Pacific, Philadelphia, American, Boston, Cincinnati, and Midwest stock exchanges, so that the brokers, specialists, and market makers can participate in other exchanges. The database technology led to the creation of a whole new financial information services industry. Many companies went into the business of developing integrated financial information services by collecting information from a variety of sources such as wire services, brokerage firms, banks, insurance companies, stock exchanges, and the government, and selling the rights to access these large data banks. Integrated Financial Information Network (IMNET) by Merrill Lynch and IBM, The Source by the Reader's Digest, Dow Jones News Retrieval Service, and the Monitor Service by Reuters are the most prominent examples. With the knowledge base technology, many systems that simulate the behavior of brokers, market specialists, and investors came into existence. A variety of investment strategies have been programmed. Not only did these systems give advice to investors and brokers, but often they were left to make investment decisions alone without human intervention. Such programmed trading by major investment houses and by insurance and pension funds received a lot of publicity and was largely blamed for the stock market crash of October 1987.

## Retailing

Retailing also was heavily impacted by data processing systems through point-of-sale systems (POS) and credit cards. POS systems cut the transaction costs by automating many of the office tasks such as invoicing, billing, inventory update, and accounting. These systems capture transactions at the point of sale, and all bookkeeping from that point on is done by the system with no human interference. The large initial investment for these systems and the subsequent drop in transaction costs changed economies of scale and created a move toward large regional and national retail outlets. Credit cards also reduced the transaction costs for consumers by supplying instant credit and a universally accepted substitute for bulky and insecure cash. Credit cards blurred the distinction between retailers and financial institutions and many retailers and manufacturers such as Sears Roebuck, Mobil Oil, and General Motors went into the financial services business, providing stiff competition to commercial banks in the area of consumer loans and services. Mobil Oil Corporation spent significant resources to build a network of POS systems connecting 3,600 service stations nationwide to its main data processing center in Kansas City, Kansas. The system not only does transaction processing and customer billing, but also provides credit information for a variety of internal and external users. With database technology came direct marketing. Large databases of consumer goods containing information about price, quality, availability, delivery time, possible uses, comparison to other goods, and many other attributes were made available to consumers. These databases ranged from simple printed catalogs to video displays and home shopping television networks. Sabre Airline Reservation System of American Airlines gained particular notoriety in this area by providing travel and flight information, booking seats, confirming reservations, billing and receiving payments for a variety of airlines and travel agents. A whole new marketing concept emerged, directed to homes with computers, allowing customers to access product databases through a computer network and order directly from the manufacturer. By matching product information to consumer profiles over large databases, the concept of targeted advertising gained momentum where product information was directed to those most likely to buy it. Even multiple descriptions of a product were developed to appeal to different customer groups in different ways and with a different message, although the product is the same. Knowledge base systems are not very common in retailing, although some isolated systems exist to give advice on real estate, automobile, and home appliance purchase decisions. Systems that will automatically develop a customer profile from previous purchasing decisions and use the profile to aid in future purchases are attempted, both to aid the customer and the salesman. Personalized advertising by altering the message for the tastes and preferences of each customer is emerging, and it requires an extensive knowledge base including not only data about consumers and products but rules and procedures to match them and connect them without writing programs for each possible match.

## Manufacturing

Data processing systems laid the foundation for robotics, especially in the automobile industry. Special-purpose robot arms repeating a simple task such as welding or painting in a controlled environment are driven by data processing systems and they are common in industry. They are also commonly used in automatic control systems, self-regulating systems, or exception reporting alarm systems in steel and nuclear industries. Database systems are commonly used in flexible manufacturing systems where all resources are shared among all the tasks to maximize resource utilization. This environment is wrought with logistics issues where a large number of resources must be managed by shifting them continually among tasks to optimize resource utilization, thus it requires large amounts of data from a variety of sources indicating the status of each resource and each task on a continuous basis. Raw materials, machines, warehouses, orders, and customers must be observed and their status and their requirements must be reported in a timely fashion to managers controlling the flexible manufacturing process. Database technology is essential for such an integrated and unpredictable reporting environment. The Management Information and Decision Support (MIDS) System of Lockheed Aircraft Manufacturing Corporation is a typical example. It has over 700 standard reports serving the needs of manufacturing and sales managers, in addition to an ad hoc querying capability of the status of all resources, production lines, aircraft in production, aircraft on order, expected delivery dates, payments received or promised, sales force distribution, sales representatives responsible for each order, and for each prospective customer, and the status and preferences of each actual or prospective customer. By 1985 MIDS had become such an important part of the corporate culture at Lockheed that the president of Lockheed-Georgia admitted that it was no longer just an accounting or manufacturing control system but it was an essential component of his strategic information sources. A similar system exists in Hughes Aircraft Company, a subsidiary of General Motors, which constantly compares manufacturing status reports against preestablished targets to detect scheduling and quality control problems as early as possible. Such exception reporting is even more critical at Buckeye Pipeline Company of Pennsylvania. This firm maintains 3,600 miles of commercial pipelines throughout the Northeast, supplying virtually all the jet fuel to many major airports. Its information system collects a variety of data about pumps, valves, flow rate, pressure, and temperature, and tries to detect leaks and security violations by comparing them to preestablished values. Knowledge base technology is essential for flexible, general-purpose robots. Robots that sense their environment and adjust to it by taking appropriate action require many flexible rules and procedures in addition to data. Such unstructured and partially programmed behavior can only be captured in a knowledge base environment. Such robots are being developed at the National Aeronautics and Space Agency (NASA) for interstellar exploration. Knowledge base technology is also useful in product design to meet customer specifications in custom-made manufacturing industries. The best-known example is XCON of Digital Equipment Corporation which designs microcomputer chips and other computer components to meet customer specifications. XCON has been used extensively in the design of VAX computers. Other examples include IDRILL of Ingersoll that assists engineers in the design of oil drilling stations, and ALADIN of Alcoa that helps metallurgists to design new aluminum alloys which will exhibit certain physical properties.

## Law and Criminal Justice

Data processing systems are used extensively for record keeping at police departments, courts, and in federal government. Not only arrests, convictions, and prison records, but also a variety of regulatory activity such as registering weapons and automobiles, recording real estate transactions, environmental pollution levels, and tax returns all require data processing systems. Processing tax returns, checking for errors, comparing a tax return with other tax returns such as the previous year's by the same taxpayer or his employer's, spouse's, landlord's or bank's tax return, and selecting some returns for audit, are all done by data processing systems. Sometimes such records are integrated under central control to allow cross-referencing and to increase flexibility to respond to a variety of unanticipated questions by utilizing database technology. The power of such integrated systems can be best understood by considering the ability to investigate an individual by cross-referencing his tax records, real estate records, automobile and weapons registrations, warranties on his appliances, arrest records, utility, telephone and cable bills, and his bank account records. The power gained by such investigative power is most visible when the threat to privacy of an individual is considered. To limit the exercise of this power by governments, insurance agencies, banks, police departments and other individuals and to protect the privacy of citizens is a major challenge in the database environment. Database technology is also critical in storing large numbers of statutes, government regulations, legal precedents, and judicial opinions, and in making them accessible to a variety of lawyers and law students for a variety of purposes. The largest of these systems is LEXIS database developed by Mead Corporation. It is accessible from most law libraries in the United States and it contains the biggest collection of legal citations, regulations, and judicial opinions both at the federal and state level. Knowledge base systems are not common in law, but many criminal law consulting systems to aid lawyers in plea bargaining, and judges in sentencing have been designed. There are also experimental systems to aid criminal investigators by developing criminal profiles and personalities and matching them against the evidence or the style of a particular crime. These types of systems have been used in identifying pathological personalities such as serial murderers.

## Medicine

Medical records have always been a bottleneck in the practice of medicine, especially in large hospitals. Data processing systems have automated storage and retrieval of medical records, smoothing hospital operations, greatly improving the relationship between medical and administrative personnel, and preventing many errors and delays in treatment. They are also used extensively to support modern diagnostic tools such as computer axial tomography (CAT) scanners and positron emission tomography (PET) scanners in converting electronic impulses to visual images. Database systems have been used extensively in pharmacology to record specifications of drugs, their effects, side effects, and interactions, and to cross reference them with customer and prescription information to select the best therapy and to prevent dangerous combinations and side effects. Knowledge base systems also found their earliest examples in medicine. MYCIN is probably the best-known commercial knowledge base system, designed to advise physicians in diagnosing infectious diseases. It has been used extensively both experimentally and clinically and was found to be an excellent aid to a physician, and often an adequate substitute for it. The PUFF (Pulmonary Function) system is similar to MYCIN but restricted to diagnosing pulmonary problems. More general medical consulting systems include CARE of Regenstrief Institute of Health Care in Indianapolis, and HELP of LDS Hospital in Salt Lake City, Utah. Both systems provide wide-ranging medical consulting in all specialties, plus pharmacology, instrumentation, diagnostic procedures, and patient monitoring.

## Political Process

Electronic voting and tallying rely on data processing systems. They are used widely in national and local elections, in Congress, and in state governments. Electronic polling is also widely practiced and its success has changed the political landscape. Polls can determine political strategies, candidates' schedules, and even voters' attitudes and behavior. No political campaign at any level is likely to proceed without extensive reliance on electronic polling. Database technology makes polling data even more useful by cross-referencing it with census data, voting patterns, past polling data, and time correlation of these data with specific political events. These systems make it possible to literally map the political landscape with respect to age, sex, occupation, income, location, ideology, etc., and to chart its course as political events influence it. Every political decision can be analyzed as to its effect on this political landscape. This technology is so influential that it actually encourages making political decisions purely on the basis of its effect on various constituencies with no general principles. It is interesting to observe that database technology is diminishing the reliance on general principles and ideologies as summary positions for certain constituencies, but encouraging "pure" politics where each decision is analyzed individually as to its effect on various constituencies. Knowledge base systems are rarely used in the political process because of the elusiveness of political issues and judgments, but the potential is enormous. Not only the systems advising political candidates and campaign managers as to the soundness and effectiveness of their decisions, but also systems advising the general public are likely to have a major impact in the political process. Political decisions are difficult and time consuming for the average citizen. It involves analyzing the individual's own interests and concerns and evaluating the alternatives presented to him on that basis. The process is made even more complex by those who are trying to influence his decisions by controlling his information sources, or by directly feeding him misleading or incorrect information. Political consulting systems can go a long way in easing this burden on voters, and may actually revolutionize representative democracies by increasing direct participation by the citizenry and reducing reliance on representatives to analyze, explain and debate complex political issues.

## Corporate Structure

Data processing systems eliminated many clerical and low-level managerial positions, since these jobs involved structured and repetitive tasks and were easy to automate. Many bookkeepers, shipping clerks, typists, receptionists, assembly line workers, shop floor workers, bank tellers, file clerks, supermarket checkout clerks, and many others have been replaced by data processing systems. Database systems were more critical for middle management, where communication and movement of information up and down the organizational hierarchy are major tasks. Database systems, and the management information systems they made possible, allowed general organization-wide access to all corporate information. The communication and information dissemination tasks of middle management were largely taken over by database systems. The filtering of information as it moves up the organizational hierarchy, and expansion and execution of decisions as they move down the hierarchy were greatly facilitated by management information systems which provided not only general querying capabilities into the organizational database, but also simple processing to aggregate and disaggregate data, to manipulate, to reorganize, and to filter data. All of these cut into middle management's responsibilities, easing the burden, cutting down the number of levels in hierarchies, and eliminating many jobs. Knowledge base systems targeted the top management, since they were best suited to support the ill-structured elusive environment of strategic management. Decision support systems created by using the knowledge base technology made it possible to capture the poorly understood and minimally structured decision processes of top managers in artificially intelligent information systems. These systems have been used to give advice in many strategic decisions involving capital budgeting, mergers and acquisitions, new product positioning, and plant location decisions. In a few cases they have replaced decision makers altogether, However, it is not difficult to look ahead and imagine the day when information systems can replace all managerial and clerical employees. The day of the corporation without employees is easy to contemplate if the substitution of capital for labor continues. The dilemmas posed by such a business world are many and complex. Moving another step further, since it is feasible for a corporation to buy all of its own stock, it is possible to imagine a company with no employees and no stockholders. A corporation with no human input, a giant corporate machine (literally) is a frightening social construct indeed. It is difficult to imagine the social consequences of such a corporate machine getting involved in the political process to further its corporate interests, like all other corporations. Those interests may not coincide with any of the human members of the society, and creation of a new political class consisting of such corporate machines would challenge all existing social institutions.

## QUESTIONS

1. Give examples of information used in a variety of managerial activities and identify components.

2. Give examples of information systems used in a variety of organizations and characterize their type.

## BIBLIOGRAPHY

Burch, J. G., Strater, F. R., Grudnitski, G. *Information Systems: Theory and Practice.* New York: John Wiley & Sons, 1983.

Estabrooks, M. *Programmed Capitalism: A Computer Mediated Global Society.* Armonk, NY: M. E. Sharp Inc., 1988.

Gray, P., King, W. R., McLean, E. R., Watson, H. J. *Management of Information Systems.* Hinesdale, ILL: The Dryden Press, 1989.

Knight, K. E., Reuben, R. M. *Organizations: An Information Systems Perspective.* New York: Wadsworth, 1979.

Senn, J. A. *Information Systems in Management.* New York: John Wiley & Sons, 1987.

Turban E., Watkins P. R. *Applied Expert Systems.* New York: North Holland, 1988.

# *Part*
# *I*

◆

# *Data Processing Systems*

Data processing systems are the earliest examples of computerized information systems. They are characterized by *files* for storing data and computer *programs* for defining procedures. These systems are not designed to be shared by a variety of users, but instead an independent stand alone-system is designed for each application. All data needs of that application are stored in its files, and all of its procedures are compiled into its programs. The files and programs of an application are rarely used by other applications unless they happen to have very similar requirements. This environment leads to a high level of duplication both of data and procedures since it is not conducive to sharing. Costly as they are to develop since they have to be custom made and existing components can not be borrowed and shared, they are efficient to execute and easy to use, precisely because of their custom-made nature. Unlike shared systems, they can be optimized to run efficiently for the only application they serve, and they can provide convenient user interfaces for the only type of user they expect.

# Chapter 2

◆

# Files

*Files* are simple reservoirs of data. Out of the four components of data (entities, attributes, values and relationships), they accommodate only the first three, assuming away relationships. Entities, attributes, and values are represented in a two-dimensional structure, called a file, where each row corresponds to an entity, each column corresponds to an attribute of that entity, and the structure is filled with the corresponding values.

---

◆ **EXAMPLE 2.1.** ◆

An employee file containing data about the employees of a company is shown below. Each row corresponds to an employee, and the columns correspond to the relevant attributes of employees such as NAME, AGE, and SALARY.

| NAME | AGE | SALARY |
|------|-----|--------|
| SMITH | 26 | 18000 |
| JONES | 38 | 42000 |
| DOE | 58 | 21000 |

EMPLOYEE

Most commercial files are large and the cost of accessing and retrieving data is considerable. Beginning students usually assume that each user in need of data merely scans the file from beginning to end in search of his data. Even with the most powerful computers such *sequential* processing of large commercial files will lead to intolerably high costs and delays. To appreciate the difficulty of sequential processing of large files one only needs to consider an unsorted phone book. The possibility of having to sequentially search a phone book to locate a given person's phone number is considered an impossibility for all practical purposes. A data item is often referred to as "inaccessible" under those circumstances since for all practical purposes and within reasonable cost restriction it is inaccessible.

To complicate matters even further, there are a variety of data requests a file is expected to accommodate. A file designed to efficiently respond to a certain type of request may not be efficient or even acceptable for another type of request. The most common type of request is, "Given an entity and attribute, find the value." However, in general, any part of the entity—attribute—value triplet may be given, and the rest requested, leading to the seven different types of requests shown in Example 2.2.

In the next two sections we will restrict ourselves to the fourth type of request, where an entity is given and all information about it is requested. The assumption is that all attributes of an entity are clustered together and once the user finds that cluster, he can easily (possibly manually) pick and choose the attributes he needs. The collection of all attribute-value pairs corresponding to an entity is called a *record,* and searching for a record corresponding to an entity is the subject of a *file search*. The entity itself is obviously outside the system and cannot be presented to guide to search. Instead, one of its attributes is selected to represent the entity. That attribute is called the *key* or *primary key* and it is required to uniquely identify each entity (see Example 2.3).

A file can be structured in a variety of ways to respond to the search requests efficiently. The structure of a file refers to the physical placement of records on the storage device, and

**EXAMPLE 2.2.**

A classification of data requests from a file leads to seven types shown below where G represents what is given and ? represents what is requested:

| | Entity | Attribute | Value |
|---|---|---|---|
| 1. | G | G | ? |
| 2. | G | ? | G |
| 3. | ? | G | G |
| 4. | G | ? | ? |
| 5. | ? | G | ? |
| 6. | ? | ? | G |
| 7. | ? | ? | ? |

The first type is the most common, where an entity and an attribute are given, and a value is requested. An example is, "What is employee SMITH's age?" where employee SMITH is an entity, and AGE is an attribute.

 **EXAMPLE 2.3.**

Social Security number is generally used as a key for an EMPLOYEE file since these numbers are chosen to be unique for each employee, and the NAME attribute is not always appropriate since more than one employee may have the same name.

the choice of additional information to be stored to aid the search. Two general file structures can be identified. *Contiguous structures* place records in neighboring locations on the device with no holes, while *dispersed structures* distribute them throughout the device. Also, *sorted files* sort records with respect to the values of the key attribute, while the *unsorted files* do not.

# File Search

Given a contiguous sorted file, a search with respect to the primary key can be conducted using three general methods. A *sequential search* requires a sequential check of each record until the requested record is located. If the file is unsorted this is the only available method. A *blocked search* is slightly more efficient. It partitions the file into blocks and does a two-stage search. In the first stage the appropriate block is located, and in the second stage the correct block is searched for the requested record. A *binary search* involves jumping to the middle of the file, checking one record, and identifying which half of the file contains the requested record. The procedure is repeated and halves the file segment to be searched at each step.

A sequential search is the least efficient of the three search strategies. It involves checking every record, starting at the beginning of the file, until the requested record is found. In Figure 2.1, for example, to find the record for "Ellen," eight records would have to be checked. For a file with $n$ records, sequential search requires on average $(n+1)/2$ records to be checked before the requested record can be found. Its inefficiency can be visualized by imagining a sequential search through the phone book, checking every entry from the beginning, to find a particular record. A typical example of a sequential search in our daily lives is the search for a parking space on the street while driving by.

A blocked search is more efficient than a sequential search; however, it requires a more complicated structure that allows a search for the correct block, and restricts the file search to within that block. Typically, a blocked search requires an additional file, called an *index file*, each record of which identifies a block of the main file. Figure 2.1 shows an index file partitioning the main file into blocks of five records. Each record in the index file points to the beginning of a block of five records and contains the last value in the block. The search is done in two stages. To find the record for "Ellen," for example, first

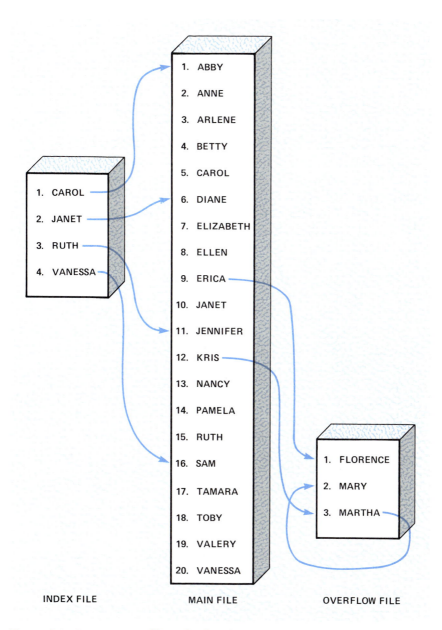

Figure 2.1. A contiguous file and related structures.

the index file is searched sequentially until a record is found with a key value past "Ellen." The first record with a key value past "Ellen" is "Janet", and consequently the record 6 in the main file identifies the beginning of the block that contains "Ellen." Ellen's record can be found by sequentially searching within that block of five records. Obviously, a blocked search requires a sorted file and an additional index file to partition the main file into blocks. It also requires a mechanism to directly move to a particular record in a file. This pointing mechanism is accomplished by storing the address of that record (called a *pointer*) and employing a storage device that can move directly to a record in a file as long as its address is known. In Figure 2.1, for example, the second record in the index file contains a pointer to the sixth record in the main file by merely storing the address "6" at the end of the second record in the index file. The blocked search is more efficient than the sequential search. Given a file with $n$ records partitioned into $k$ blocks, on average $(k + 1)/2 + (n/k + 1)/2$ records will have to be checked to find a particular record. The first term refers to the search of the index file which contains $k$ records, each corresponding to a block. The second term refers to the search within the correct block which contains approximately $n/k$ records. A typical example of a blocked search in our daily lives is searching for a book in the library, where each shelf corresponds to a block, and the shelf labels constitute an index file. The main file is the library itself, each record is a book, and the key attribute is the call number.

A binary search is even more efficient than a blocked search, however, it requires the ability to find the middle point of a given file segment. It starts with the complete file and halves the search space at each step by jumping to the middle of the file comparing the key value to the requested record, and restricting the search to the relevant half. A binary search for "Ellen" in Figure 2.1, for example, would check Janet's record first. Since "Ellen" comes before "Janet," the search will be restricted to the first half of the file, that is, records 1–9. At the second step Carol's record will be checked and the search will be further restricted to the records 6–9. The search continues until the record is found or the search space reduces to 0 records, in which case the requested record is decided to be nonexistent. Given a file with $n$ records, it takes a maximum of $\log_2 n$ records to be checked to find a particular record. This formula follows from the fact that the search space is halved at each step. The closest we come in our daily lives to doing a binary search is in using the phone book or dictionary. Humans are actually more efficient than a binary search since they estimate the approximate location of a record (e.g., the name "Orman" being slightly after the middle in a phone book) and they jump to that approximate location directly rather than the middle of the file.

## File Maintenance

Files are not static structures. New records are constantly added to a file, and old records are deleted or modified. The major disadvantage of a sorted contiguous file is the difficulty of maintenance. To insert a record, one needs to move a large number of records to preserve the contiguity and the sort. To delete a record, again, a large number of records have to be moved at great cost, or contiguity must be sacrificed. To solve the insertion problem, a new file called the *overflow file* is created. The new records are placed in the overflow file in order of arrival without disturbing the main file. Pointers are used to indicate the correct position of these new records in the main file. A *pointer* is merely an address of a record. A *pointer field* is an address stored in a record indicating the position of another record, and it provides a direct access path from one record to another. The correct position of an overflow record is indicated by a pointer from the main file to the overflow file. It links the record in the main file that should directly precede the new record, to the new record itself residing in the overflow file. The new record "Florence" for example in Figure 2.1 is pointed to by "Erica", since "Florence" comes immediately

after "Erica" in alphabetical order. Overflow records themselves may have pointers to accommodate the possibility of
more than one overflow record competing for the same position
in the main file. "Mary" and "Martha" both come immediately
after "Kris" in alphabetical order, but only one pointer field
exists in the record for "Kris". Consequently, a chain is created
by linking "Kris" to "Martha" since "Martha" comes before
"Mary", and by linking Martha's record to Mary within the
overflow file. Searching this complete structure requires an
occasional jump to the overflow file and back to the main file
to follow the alphabetical sequence. For each record checked
in the main file, its overflow pointer field needs to be checked
to see if the next record is in the overflow file. If the field is
empty the search continues in the main file. If the field is not
empty, then the search must check the overflow record pointed
by the pointer field and return to the main file to continue. For
each record checked in the overflow file, the search has to check
its overflow pointer to see if there are other records in
the overflow file to be checked before returning. When an
empty pointer field is found, the search returns to the main
file. The procedure to accomplish this search is shown in
Figure 2.2.

The blocked search with an overflow file is done in a similar
fashion by possibly jumping to the overflow file for each record
checked within the search block. Binary search is slightly different since the overflow file does not have to be checked until
the end of the search. If the file segment to be searched is
reduced to a single record and the requested record has not
been found then the possibility of residence in the overflow file
is investigated. There is no need to search the whole overflow
file, but only to follow the pointer from the last record checked
since the relevant file size has been reduced to one record, and
the relevant overflow records are the ones that are connected
to it. For example, to retrieve "Florence" through a binary
search, the main file search is completed until "Erika" is
the only record left in the search area, then the pointer
from "Erika" is followed to the overflow area to locate
"Florence."

```
loop1:
 check the next record
 if found  print "found"
          exit loop1
 else
  check its pointer field
  if empty iterate loop1
  else loop2:
       check the pointed overflow record
       if found  print "found"
                 exit loop1
       else check its pointer field
           if empty iterate loop1
           else iterate loop2
       end loop2
 end loop1
```

Figure 2.2. The sequential search of a sorted contiguous file with overflow.

## Dispersed Files

The records of a file do not have to occupy contiguous spaces, but may be dispersed throughout the storage device. The records of a *dispersed file* have to be linked together with pointers from each record to the next, creating a chain. These structures are called *chains* or *linked lists*. The major advantage of a chain is the ease of maintenance. The insertion of new records can be accomplished by placing the new record in the first available slot and adjusting the pointers to include the new record in the appropriate place in the chain. Deletion is also simple, involving only the modification of some pointers to exclude a record from the chain. The disadvantage of a chain is the large cost of following pointers, usually over large distances, on the storage device. Searching dispersed files involves following pointers from one record to the next. Blocked search is possible by creating an index file that points to the beginning of each block as in contiguous files. Binary search with dispersed files is not practical.

A major use of the chain structure actually involves contiguous files. When a contiguous file is searched with respect to an attribute other than its key it actually behaves like a dispersed file and a chain structure is in order. So far we have looked at searches with respect to the key (i.e., given the entity, find the corresponding record). A search with respect to an attribute other than the key precludes all the strategies developed so far. An attribute other than the key used for a file search is called a *secondary key*. A file searched with respect to a secondary key behaves like a dispersed file since it is not sorted with respect to the secondary key. A chain structure linking the records in a sorted order of secondary key values is necessary to do efficient searches. Figure 2.3 shows the PART file containing information about the parts used in a manufacturing environment. The file is sorted with respect to the "part number" key attribute, with an overflow area to accommodate the insertions. So far the structure cannot efficiently respond to questions involving the secondary key of "price," for example, "find all parts priced under five dollars." To respond to questions of that type, a chain structure is created connecting the records in order of the price values. A sequential search with respect to price merely follows the price pointer. A blocked search requires the creation of an index pointing to the beginning of each stock within the chain structure. An index file pointing to blocks of five is shown in Figure 2.3. As in Figure 2.1, each index record contains the last value in the block but points to the beginning of the block.

## File Optimization

*File optimization* is a major area of study in information systems. It deals with the discovery of optimum structures for each environment. Typical questions are optimum search

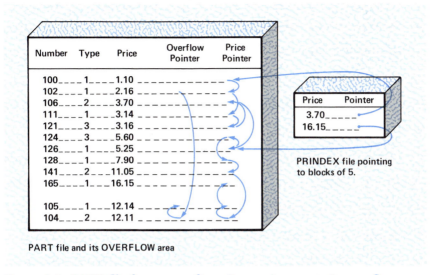

PART file and its OVERFLOW area

Figure 2.3. PART file for a manufacturing environment, its overflow area and overflow pointers, a chain for the price attribute and the price index file PRINDEX.

strategies, optimum block size, and the optimum timing of file reorganization. The last issue relates to the timing of overhauls of contiguous structures to alleviate inefficiencies resulting from insertions and deletions. Insertions may lead to a large overflow file, and deletions may lead to holes in the file, each being a major source of inefficiency. The cost of these inefficiencies has to be balanced against the cost of an overhaul that reoptimizes the structure by resorting and reblocking. The optimization of dispersed structures must deal with the optimum number of pointers, the direction of the pointers, and blocking factors.

## QUESTIONS

1. Given the PART file of Figure 2.3, write a computer program to do a binary search to find a record associated with

a given part number. The part number to be found should be established interactively. Once the record is found, print the number, type, and price of the requested part.
*Hint:* Pay extra attention to the first and last record in the file, and to the requests for nonexisting records.

2. Repeat Question 1 for sequential and blocked search strategies. Count the number of records checked to respond to each request.

3. Write a program that keeps track of the number of records checked to respond to each request, and then compute an average number of records checked for each search strategy. Use these averages to argue the relative efficiency of each search strategy.

4. Modify the program in Question 1 to also find all the parts that are similar to the requested part as possible substitutes. The program should print their numbers, types, and prices. A part is considered to be similar to another part if it is of the same type and the price difference is less than 5 dollars.
*Hint:* Use the price chain and the price index.

## BIBLIOGRAPHY

Martin, J. *Computer Database Organization.* Englewood Cliffs, NJ: Prentice-Hall, 1977.

Wiederhold, G. *Database Design.* New York: McGraw-Hill, 1977.

---

*Chapter 3*

---

◆

# File Relationships

Files are not independent, solitary structures. They are often related to each other, and those relationships are often a critical part of the data.

◆──┤ **EXAMPLE 3.1.** ├──◆

Given a PART file and a SUPPLIER file for a manufacturing environment containing information about parts and suppliers of those parts, respectively. The two files are related to each other in the sense that certain parts are supplied by certain suppliers. Consequently, for each record in one file there are associated records in the other file.

In a data processing environment, these relationships are often ignored by placing all data needs of an application in the same file. This approach allows the optimization of a file structure for a given application. The placement of all data needs of an application in the same file is usually done at the time of file creation, but sometimes it is delayed until a request comes in. Sort-Merge procedures of Chapter 4 are geared toward combining all data needs of a request in one file after the request is received. As one moves toward a database environment and allows more and more sharing, such clustering of data in one file for each application becomes less and less feasible. As we will see in Part II, the database environment requires access in a variety of ways simultaneously to serve a variety of applications. A fixed structure for each application is not efficient, since it duplicates all the common components, and creating these structures after a request comes in is not efficient, since it has to be repeated for every request. Consequently a move toward a more shared environment requires a separate implementation of the file relationships.

◆ **EXAMPLE 3.2.** ◆

The suppliers of each part and their associated information can be included in the PART file. This structure would be very efficient in finding the suppliers of each part, but useless in finding the parts supplied by each supplier. A symmetrical structure to also include the part information in the supplier file would lead to large-scale duplication. To leave the two files separate would require an appropriate merging of them for each request and this procedure would have to be repeated for many similar requests. Neither of these strategies is acceptable in a shared environment.

## Types of Relationships

There are three types of relationships between two files. A one-to-one (1:1) relationship is when each record in one file is related to exactly one record in the other. A many-to-one relationship (M:1) is when each record in the first file is related to exactly one record in the second, but each record in the second file may be related to zero, one, or more records in the first. A many-to-many (M:M) relationship is when for each record in one file there may be zero, one, or more related records in the other.

◆ **EXAMPLE 3.3.** ◆

Given the manufacturing environment of Example 3.1, the three types of relationships are shown below.

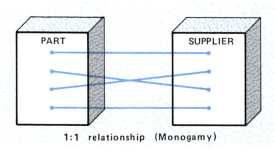

1:1 relationship (Monogamy)

Each part has exactly one supplier, and each supplier supplies exactly one part.

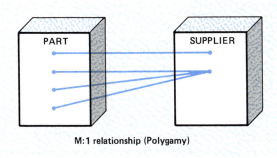

M:1 relationship (Polygamy)

**EXAMPLE 3.3.** *(Continued)*

Each part has exactly one supplier, but each supplier may supply zero, one, or more parts.

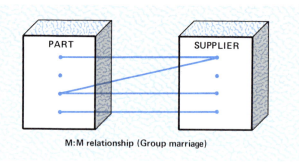

M:M relationship (Group marriage)

There are no restrictions on the number of suppliers supplying a part, or on the number of parts supplied by a supplier.

The direction of a M:1 relationship is important since a M:1 relationship is different from a 1:M relationship. The file on the 1 side has exactly one record for each record of the other file, but not vice versa. In a M:1 relationship, the file on the 1 side is called a *child* file and the file on the M side is called a *parent* file. They are also referred to as the *member* file and the *owner* file, respectively. In Example 3.3, the PART file is the child (member) file, and the SUPPLIER is the parent (owner) file.

## *Implementation*

The distinction among the three types of relationships is important because they lead to different implementations at different levels of efficiency. M:M is the most general structure and its implementation is the least efficient. If one can assume a 1:1 or a M:1 relationship, a much more efficient implementation can be achieved. However, if the assumption is violated, the violators cannot be included in the structure and must be treated as special cases at great cost.

A 1:1 relationship is easily implemented by adding one pointer per record, pointing to the related record in the other file.

◆ **EXAMPLE 3.4.** ◆

A 1:1 relationship between the PART and SUPPLIER files is implemented with one pointer per record.

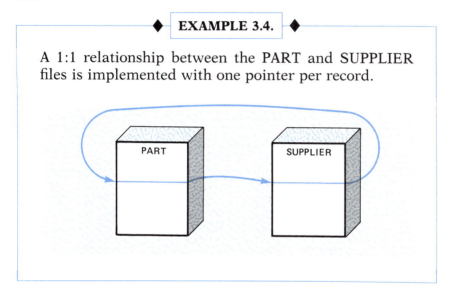

A M:1 relationship obviously may require more than one pointer per record in one file, each pointing to one of the associated pointers. However, a structure with multiple pointers is not desirable for two reasons. First, a variable number of pointers per record requires a variable-size record, which in turn requires markers to indicate the beginning and end of each record. These markers create overhead and deteriorate the efficiency of the system. More importantly, at the time of creation, the maximum number of possible pointers is not known, and it is not clear how much space should be allocated to each record. No matter how much space is allocated (thereby creating empty space and inefficiency), it is always possible that one record may exceed all expectations and overflow the space, requiring exceptional treatment and leading to further inefficiency. Consequently, a variable number of pointers per record is usually not a desirable option. Instead, M:1 relationships are usually implemented with a "ring" structure where the record on the 1 side points to the first record on the M side. The related records on the M side are connected to each other in a chain, and the last record in the chain points back to the record on the 1 side.

◆ EXAMPLE 3.5. ◆

A M:1 relationship between the PART and SUPPLIER files is implemented as a ring.

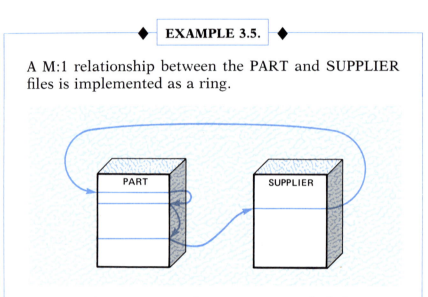

It is simple to traverse this structure to find the parts supplied by a supplier. One follows the pointer from the supplier record into the PART file and follows the chain until the end. Each record on the chain is a part supplied by that supplier. To search in the opposite direction is slightly more complicated. To find the supplier of a part, the chain has to be followed until it leaves the PART file and returns to the SUPPLIER file. The record found at the end of the ring is the supplier requested. Obviously, a mechanism is needed to distinguish the pointers within the file from a pointer between files, to notice the end of the ring. The ring structure is by definition circular and unless the pointers are distinguished the search may continue indefinitely, or a PART record may be confused with a SUPPLIER record.

A M:M relationship is the most general and the most difficult to implement. It cannot be implemented with rings since rings will intersect and make it impossible to stay on one chain while searching. Every intersection will involve multiple chains passing through a record and picking the right chain to follow requires the extensive overhead of labeling. Instead, M:M relationships are implemented by creating a new file called an *intersection* file. This file contains a record for every related pair of PART-SUPPLIER records.

◆ **EXAMPLE 3.6.** ◆

An intersection file containing a record for each related pair of PART-SUPPLIER records is shown below.

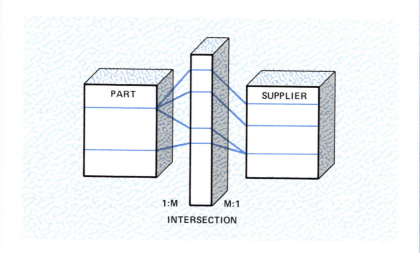

The use of intersection file manages to split an M:M relationship into two 1:M relationships. Both relationships have the INTERSECTION file on the M side since for each part record there are multiple intersection records each corresponding to a supplier of the part, and for each supplier record there are multiple intersection records each corresponding to a part supplied by that supplier. Once the M:M relationship is split into

**EXAMPLE 3.6.** *(Continued)*

two M:1 relationships, each M:1 relationship can be implemented using ring structures. This is the most commonly used structure to implement a M:M relationship.

◆ **EXAMPLE 3.7.** ◆

The relationship between the PART and SUPPLIER files can be implemented using an intersection file and two ring structures.

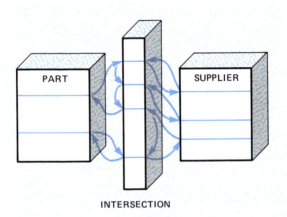

INTERSECTION

The intersection file contains no information other than two pointers per record, one pointer corresponding to chains starting in the PART file, and another pointer corresponding to chains starting in the SUPPLIER file. To traverse this structure, two rings have to be followed. To find all the suppliers of a part, the search starts at the part record, follows the chain into the INTERSECTION file, and continues through the chain until it returns to the PART file. Each record on this chain corresponds to a supplier of the part. To find the supplier corresponding to an intersection record, the second chain is followed until it leaves the INTERSEC-TION file and points to the SUPPLIER file. The SUP-PLIER record at the end of the chain is the supplier corresponding to the intersection record. This process must be repeated for every record on the first chain to find all suppliers of the part. The search for all parts supplied by a supplier is similar in the opposite direction.

## QUESTIONS

1.  Given the PART and SUPPLIER files with the structure shown in Example 3.7, write a program that receives a part number interactively, and finds all suppliers who supply that part.

2.  Write a similar computer program for the structure in Example 3.5.

## BIBLIOGRAPHY

Martin, J. *Computer Data Base Organization*. Englewood Cliffs, NJ: Prentice-Hall, 1977.

Wiederhold, G. *Database Design*. New York: McGraw-Hill, 1977.

# Chapter 4

♦

# Programs

Procedures are generally expressed as computer programs. There are many commercial programming languages to facilitate the expression of procedures as computer programs in unambiguous and machine executable form. Languages such as **BASIC, FORTRAN, COBOL, PL1,** and **PASCAL** are widely available on practically all computers, and they are often standardized across machines for easy transportability. All of these languages are based on the Von Neumann concept of assignment of values to named storage spaces called *variables.* These stored values are manipulated one at a time until a desired effect is achieved. There are three major constructs to manipulate the stored values in all popular programming languages: sequential instructions, conditionals, and loops. In addition, there are constructs to facilitate the interaction of the program with its environment; these are called input-output instructions.

## Sequential Instructions

*Sequential instructions* are assignment commands to be executed in sequence. They change the contents of a named storage space, called a *variable,* either directly or through arithmetic and logical operations.

◆ **EXAMPLE 4.1.** ◆

Assignment commands assign a value to a named variable:

A = 10    will store the value 10 in a variable named A.

A = B + C*(D − E)/F**2

will store the value $B + C \times (D − E)/F^2$ in A.

In addition to arithmetic operations, a number of standard functions are provided by each programming language:

A = SQRT(INT(LOG(B + SINE(C))))    will store the square root of the integer part of natural logarithm of B + SINE(C).

Storing a value in a variable destroys its previous contents, but using a variable in an expression does not change its value.

## *Conditionals*

*Conditionals* are instructions to be executed only under certain conditions. They are used to express branching and alternative procedures within the logic of the program. The conditions are merely tests on the contents of the variables. The general structure of a conditional is:

IF cond THEN ____    ELSE ____

where an instruction is executed only if the condition is true, and another is executed otherwise; or

```
IF cond
   ≡
ELSE
   ≡
END
```

where a set of instructions is executed if a condition is true, and a different set of instructions is executed if it is false. The conditions may be simple tests involving comparison operations =, ≠, <, >, ≤, ≥, or they may be more complex involving multiple conditions combined with logical operations such as AND and OR. The conditionals may be nested within each other into arbitrary levels to express more complex procedures.

◆ **EXAMPLE 4.2.** ◆

The following example shows the interest rates paid by a bank on savings and checking accounts depending on the balance of the account:

```
IF TYPE="SAVINGS"
  IF BALANCE<100 THEN INTEREST=0.00
  IF BALANCE≥100 AND BALANCE<1000 THEN
                              INTEREST=0.06
  IF BALANCE≥1000 THEN INTEREST=0.09
ELSE
  INTEREST=0.00
END
```

## Loops

*Loops* are instructions to be executed repeatedly until an exit condition is satisfied. There are three general methods to express the exit condition. The loop may be terminated when a condition holds, it may be terminated when a condition fails, or it may be terminated when a condition set is exhausted. The three structures are shown below:

```
DO UNTIL cond
     ≡
END
DO WHILE cond
     ≡
END
DO FOR I=1 To 10
     ≡
END
```

Two other instructions are used to change the normal execution of a loop. The EXIT command directly exits the loop, and the ITERATE command moves the control to the DO command for the next iteration. The EXIT command can be used to jump out of any block such as IF-END or DO-END.

◆ **EXAMPLE 4.3.** ◆

The following program computes the sum of all even integers under 100 unle⁻s the sum exceeds 1000:

```
DO FOR I=1 TO 100
     IF INT(I/2)=0 THEN A=A+I
     IF A>1000 THEN EXIT
END
```

It is also possible to block sequential instructions without looping and use EXIT command to leave the block at an arbitrary point:

```
DO
     ≡
     EXIT
     ≡
END
```

## *Input-Output*

*Input-output* instructions facilitate the interaction between the procedures and their environment. Procedure may receive data from users or files, and provide data to them. INPUT command is used to receive data and PRINT is used to provide data.

---

◆ **EXAMPLE 4.4.** ◆

INPUT A,B    receives values for variables A and B from user in that order.

INPUT A,B FROM F    receives values for variables A and B from the next record in file F. It will read from the first two fields in that order.

PRINT A,B    will print the values associated with the variables A and B to the user. It will print them in that order in two separate columns of appropriate width.

PRINT A,B INTO F    will print the values associated with the variables A and B into the file F. It will print them in that order in two separate fields into the next record of F.

Printing a single line or record can be split into multiple PRINT statements as follows:

```
PRINT A,
PRINT B
```

will have the same effect as PRINT A, B

## Arrays

An *array* is merely a naming mechanism that facilitates reference to storage locations by numbers rather than separate names. This mechanism is useful in repeating the same operation for a number of variables without repeating the procedure. A one-dimensional array allows variables to be grouped into an array A and referred to as A(1), A(2), etc. It is sometimes called a *vector of variables*. A two-dimensional array is called a matrix and allows naming with two arguments such as A(1,1), A(1,2), etc. It can be viewed as a table where A(I,J) refers to the element located on the Ith row and Jth column.

**EXAMPLE 4.5.**

Given a two-dimensional array A(M,N), computing and printing the column totals requires looping and arrays:

```
≡
DO FOR I=1 to M
     DO FOR J=1 to N
          TOTAL (J)=TOTAL(J)+A(I,J)
     END
     PRINT TOTAL(J),
END
```

## Sorting

*Sorting* is the task of rearranging the items in an array or file in a particular sequence. It is an excellent example of all programming tools covered in this chapter. All sort procedures involve comparing selected items and exchanging them if they are found to be in the wrong order. There are many strategies to do sorting efficiently without comparing every item to every other. The most famous of these strategies is the "bubble" sort which compares every item to only the items that come after it.

◆ **EXAMPLE 4.6.** ◆

The following program sorts an array A(N) in ascending order by comparing every item to every other. This is conceptually the simplest but the least efficient sort procedure:

```
DO FOR I=1 to N
    DO FOR J=1 to N
        IF I>J AND A(I)<A(J)
            T=A(I)
            A(I)=A(J)
            A(J)=T
        END
    END
END
```

A more efficient program called "bubble sort" compares each item only to the items below it:

```
DO FOR I=1 TO N
    DO J=I+1 TO N
        IF A(I)>A(J)
            T=A(I)
            A(I)=A(J)
            A(J)=T
        END
    END
END
```

Sorting files is a more complicated task since they reside on secondary storage devices and each comparison requires retrieval of two records, and each exchange requires the rewrite of two records. Sequential files that cannot be read randomly cannot use the above algorithms. They utilize sequential sort algorithms, the most common of which involves three files. It reads from the file to be sorted, and writes partially sorted segments into two separate files. The process continues by switching the input and output files until the sort is complete.

◆ **EXAMPLE 4.7.** ◆

The following program shows one step of the sequential sort algorithm partially sorting FILE1 into FILE2 and FILE3:

```
INPUT B FROM FILE1
PRINT B INTO FILE2
INPUT C FROM FILE1
PRINT C INTO FILE3
DO UNTIL END OF FILE1
  INPUT A FROM FILE1
  IF B<C
    IF B<A AND A<C THEN PRINT A INTO FILE2
                   ELSE PRINT A INTO FILE3
  ELSE
    IF C<A AND A<B THEN PRINT A INTO FILE3
                   ELSE PRINT A INTO FILE2
  END
END
```

The basic idea in this program is to create sorted segments of the file. The objective is to maximize the size

**EXAMPLE 4.7.** *(Continued)*

of each sorted segment. The program reads records from FILE1 and inserts them into FILE2 or FILE3 depending on which sequence it fits into. If the new record fits into the ascending order in both files, it is inserted into the file with larger last value to keep the other file in sequence as long as possible. If the new record fits into the ascending order in neither file then it is inserted again into the file with larger last value, again to maximize the chances of the other file continuing in sequence. This program will result in the following files FILE2 and FILE3 given the following FILE1:

| FILE1 | FILE2 | FILE3 |
|-------|-------|-------|
| 8 | 8 | 5 |
| 5 | 2 | 6 |
| 6 | 9 | 7 |
| 7 | | 11 |
| 2 | | 13 |
| 11 | | |
| 9 | | |
| 13 | | |

FILE2 and FILE3 are merely combined to form the new partially sorted FILE1, and the procedure is repeated until the file is completely sorted.

## Merging

The most common problem of a data processing environment involves the merging of two sorted files by locating the matching records.

◆ **EXAMPLE 4.8.** ◆

A simple example of merging involves a banking environment that maintains the following files:

ACCOUNT(ano, balance)

which contains the account number and the balance of each savings account in the bank.

TRANSACTION(tno, ano, amount)

which contains the transaction number, account number and the amount of each transaction, i.e., deposits or withdrawals.

The merging problem is merely locating all the transactions effecting each account and updating the account balance. Assuming both files are sorted with respect to account numbers and there is exactly one transaction per account, the following program updates the account balances by creating a new updated NACCOUNT file, and also prints an account report.

```
DO UNTIL END OF ACCOUNT
  INPUT ANO, BALANCE FROM ACCOUNT
  INPUT TNO, AN, AMOUNT FROM TRANSACTION
  NB=BALANCE+AMOUNT
  PRINT ANO, NB INTO NACCOUNT
  PRINT ANO, BALANCE, AMOUNT, NB
END
```

In general, there are multiple or possibly zero transactions for each account, and this more general program is left as an exercise. With direct access files where every record is directly accessible without moving sequentially, the account file can be updated in place without creating a new account file in each period as follows:

**EXAMPLE 4.8.** *(Continued)*

```
DO UNTIL END OF ACCOUNT
  INPUT ANO, BALANCE FROM ACCOUNT A
  INPUT TNO, AN, AMOUNT FROM TRANSACTION
  NB=BALANCE+AMOUNT
  PRINT ANO, NB INTO ACCOUNT A
  PRINT ANO, BALANCE,AMOUNT,NB
END
```

where a record can be named (as in **A**) and accessed directly after being named.

## Basic

BASIC is one of the simplest commercial programming languages and differs from the stylized language in only a few significant commands. BASIC does not support the block structure of the stylized language. IF-ELSE-END structure has to be improvised by placing the complete structure on one line as:

```
IF cond THEN -\-\- ELSE -\-\-
```

Looping constructs are similar to the stylized language:

```
UNTIL cond
    ≡
NEXT

WHILE cond
    ≡
NEXT

FOR I=P TO Q
    ≡
NEXT I
```

The EXIT and ITERATE commands are not available, but the control has to be transferred explicitly with a GOTO ln command where ln is a line number. All lines have to be numbered, ordinarily by multiples of 10. String variables and arrays have to be declared before use.

VARIABLE A CHAR(10)

declares A as a string variable of 10 characters, and

DIM A(10,20)

declares A as a $10 \times 20$ array.

All other instructions are the same as the stylized language except for a variety of file structures provided. The sequential files are accessed in the same manner as the stylized language but they have to be opened and assigned numbers. The INPUT and PRINT commands can only refer to them using their numbers. The merging of two files is accomplished as follows, given

ACCOUNT(account number, balance)
TRANSACTION(transaction number, account number, amount)

and assuming exactly one transaction per account, and both files sorted with respect to account numbers:

```
 10    OPEN ACCOUNT FOR INPUT AS FILE 1
 20    OPEN "TRANSACTION" FOR INPUT AS FILE 2
 30    OPEN "NACCOUNT" FOR OUTPUT AS FILE 3
 40    L1:INPUT #1, ANO, BAL
 50    INPUT #2, TNO, AN, AMOUNT
 60    IF EOF(1) THEN STOP
 70    NB=BALANCE+AMOUNT
 80    PRINT #3, ANO, NB
 90    PRINT ANO, BALANCE, AMOUNT, NB
100    GOTO L1
110    END
```

Direct access files are provided by *virtual arrays* which are files that are viewed and accessed as arrays although they reside on secondary storage devices. The file merge problem of the banking environment is accomplished as follows using virtual array files:

```
 10   OPEN "ACCOUNT" AS FILE 1, VIRTUAL
 20   OPEN "TRANSACTION" AS FILE 2, VIRTUAL
 30   DIM #1,ACCOUNT(1000,2)
 40   DIM #2,TRANSACTION(1000,3)
 50   FOR I=1 TO 1000
 60    B=ACCOUNT(I,2)+TRANSACTION(I,3)
 70    ACCOUNT (I,2)=B
 80    PRINT ACCOUNT (I,1), ACCOUNT(I,3),
                            TRANSACTION(I,3),B
 90   NEXT I
100   END
```

## *Pascal*

The programming language **PASCAL** is similar to the stylized language except that all variables and arrays have to be declared, and all files have to be opened. All blocks are characterized by **BEGIN** and **END** commands including the conditionals and loops. Conditionals are of the form:

```
IF cond THEN
     BEGIN
         ≡
     END
ELSE
     BEGIN
         ≡
     END
```

Loops follow one of the following types:

```
WHILE cond DO
    BEGIN
         ≡
    END
UNTIL cond DO
    BEGIN
         ≡
    END
FOR I=P TO Q DO
    BEGIN
         ≡
    END
```

Sequential files are accessed using the commands

$$GET(F) \quad \text{and} \quad PUT(F)$$

which correspond to INPUT and PRINT, respectively. A buffer variable F↑ contains what has been read from the file, or what is to be written into the file. The file merge problem is solved as follows:

```
UNTIL EOF(ACCOUNT) DO
BEGIN
  GET (ACCOUNT)
  GET (TRANSACTION)
  NB:=ACCOUNT↑.BALANCE+TRANSACTION↑.AMOUNT
  NACCOUNT↑.ANO:=ACCOUNT↑.ANO
  NACCOUNT↑.BALANCE:=NB
  PUT (NACCOUNT)
  WRITELN (ACCOUNT↑.ANO,ACCOUNT↑.BALANCE,
                    TRANSACTION↑.AMOUNT,NB)
END
```

Direct access files are accessed using pointer variables containing the address of a record. If Pt is a pointer variable, Pt↑

returns the record pointed by Pt. The file merge problem is solved as follows:

```
UNTIL EOF(ACCOUNT) DO
BEGIN
  GET (ACCOUNT)
  GET (TRANSACTION)
  NB:=ACCOUNT↑.BALANCE+TRANSACTION↑.AMOUNT
  ACCOUNT↑.BALANCE:=NB
  WRITELN (ACCOUNT↑.ANO,ACCOUNT↑BALANCE,
                     TRANSACTION↑.AMOUNT,NB)
  PUT (ACCOUNT)
END
```

# QUESTIONS

1. Given the following sequential files:
   ACCOUNT (account number, account type, balance) sorted with respect to account numbers,
   TRANSACTION (transaction number, account number, amount) also sorted with respect to account numbers, and
   INTEREST (account type, interest rate) containing interest rate associated with each account type. Write a program to update the account balances and to print a bank statement containing the account number, the old balance, the transaction amounts and the new balance for each account. The new balance should be computed as:

   New balance = old balance + old balance × interet rate +
   $\Sigma$ transaction amounts for that account

   The report should consist of four columns, with multiple transactions corresponding to an account listed vertically. A final row of the report should contain the column totals for old balances, transactions and new balances. Example 4.8 solves this problem in its first program, assuming exactly one transaction per account, no interest, and no totals. Your program should relax these assumptions.

2. Repeat Question 1 for direct access files.

## BIBLIOGRAPHY

Ageloff, R., Mojena, R. *Applied Basic Programming,* Belmont, CA: Wadsworth Inc., 1980.

Conway, R. W., Gries, D., Zimmerman, E. L. *A Primer on Pascal.* Cambridge, MA: Winthrop, 1981.

## Chapter 5

♦

# Systems Analysis

An information system may contain a large number of procedures, and they are rarely independent of each other. *Systems analysis* is the study of their relationship to each other and to the data. Systems science always emphasizes the relationships of components to each other as opposed to the nature of individual components, and the analysis of information systems is no exception. Examining the relationships among programs representing procedures, and their relationship to files containing data is the first step in studying an information system. It is also the first step in designing a new system since information system design has to start with an understanding of the system envisioned by the end users. The tools are the same whether the task is to describe an existing system or to specify an envisioned system. The tools can be characterized as communication tools between the end users and analysts, and also among analysts. Analysts are charged with the task of describing the system (actual or imagined) in unambiguous terms and in sufficient detail for the implementors who have little understanding of the organization that utilizes the information produced. Implementors in turn are expected to automate the specified functions using their technical expertise. Analysts, then, are facilitators of communication between the end users with organizational knowledge, and implementors with technical knowledge. The analyst positions are critical for the success of an organization, and analysts need to have both organizational and technical skills to move comfortably in both circles. The two most common tools used by analysts are data flow diagrams and specification models.

## Data Flow Diagrams

Data Flow Diagrams (DFD) are excellent graphical tools to describe information systems at high levels of abstraction. They can be used in multiple levels of abstraction where each level contains more detail than the previous, until each component is small enough to be programmed directly in a stylized programming language or described unambiguously to an implementor. DFDs are built from four simple components. A square represents an external entity, a vertical rectangle stands for a procedure, a horizontal open-ended rectangle represents a data file, and arrows indicate data flows. *External entities* are things outside the system but interact with the system through information exchange. Customers, stockholders, creditors, and managers are all external entities. External entities do not have to be external to the organization, but only to the information system. Procedures and data are the two major components of any information system as discussed in Chapter 1. *Data flows* represent the interaction among all these components, since all interaction can be characterized as data exchange. All components are labeled by appropriate names in a DFD. It is critical to pick descriptive and concise names for effective communication. Procedures names are always verbs since they correspond to actions to be taken, while all other names are nouns describing either data or entities.

---

♦ **EXAMPLE 5.1.** ♦

The following DFD (Figure 5.1) shows a customer opening a savings account in a bank:

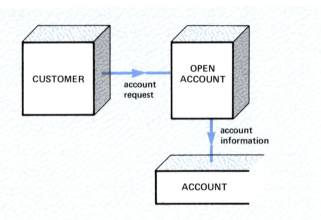

Figure 5.1.

The information about the new account comes into the system from the external entity CUSTOMER and placed into the ACCOUNT file as permanent data. The procedure OPEN ACCOUNT receives the customer information and transforms it into the appropriate form and places it in the right place in the file.

---

Specifying a large-scale system using DFDs is a painstaking task and requires great skill. DFDs for organizational systems tend to be quite large, and a systematic approach is needed for completeness and accuracy. There are two steps necessary before starting to draw large-scale DFDs. The first step in all system description involves the identification of the external entities. They are relatively simple to identify since they exist outside the system and exchange information with it. Typical external entities in a bank environment are customers, managers, clerks, government, and stockholders. The second step in preparation for drawing DFDs is the identification of all inputs and outputs exchanged with each external entity. Typical inputs from customers are requests for new accounts, deposits, withdrawals, loan applications, and loan payments. Typical outputs to customers are receipts, payments, quarterly reports, and credit reports. It is important to note that all relevant inputs and outputs are information, not physical goods. In a bank environment this distinction may not be critical, but in general DFDs are only concerned with the flow of information, not the flow of physical entities. Drawing the data flow diagram always starts with an external entity and follows an input throughout the system indicating the procedures and files it goes through until it leaves the system as an output or moves into a file. All procedures along its path are analyzed next to insure all their inputs are provided correctly, and all of their outputs are followed through the system, creating new procedures and files. This process is repeated for each external entity and each of their inputs. The resulting complete DFD is called the *top-level DFD*.

◆ **EXAMPLE 5.2.** ◆

The following DFD shows one external entity and one of its inputs followed through the system (Figure 5.2):

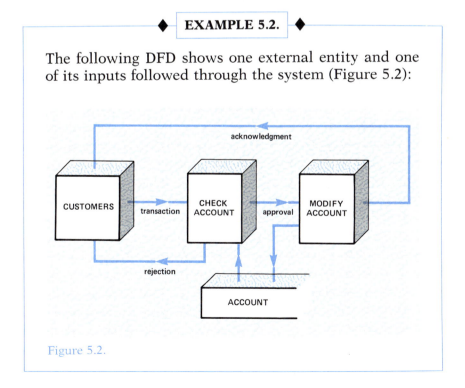

Figure 5.2.

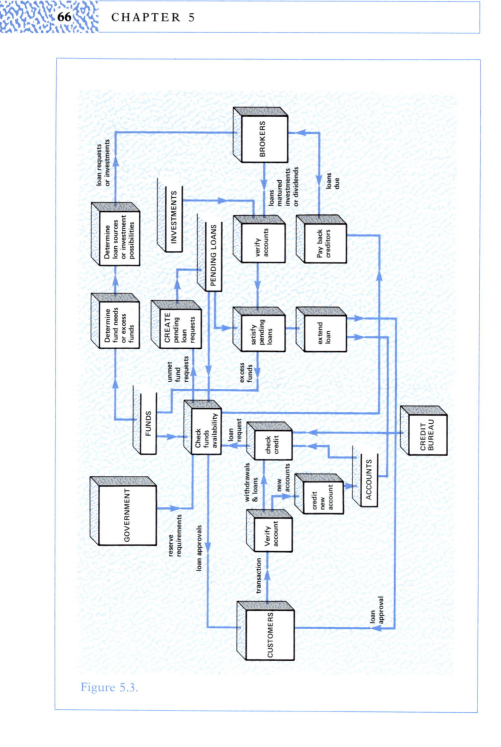

Figure 5.3.

♦ **EXAMPLE 5.3.** ♦

The DFD on page 66 (Figure 5.3) is the complete top-level DFD for the bank environment, which serves its customers with accounts and loans on the one hand, and competes for funds and investments in the marketplace on the other.

Reading a complete DFD is similar to drawing a new one. The process starts with an external entity and an input, and the arrows are followed through the system until they leave the system and reach another external entity or disappear into a file. The process should be repeated for every input from every external entity, and continue with every arrow leaving a file. This process guarantees that every arrow is checked for correctness, and all arrows leaving an external entity or file are checked for completeness. Reading a DFD requires checking its correctness and completeness at every step.

♦ **EXAMPLE 5.4.** ♦

The following DFD describes a distributorship environment with inventory (Figure 5.4).

The top-level DFD is only the first step in creating a complete description of an information system. The procedures of a top-level DFD are ambiguous and too large to be described completely in a simple English sentence or simple stylized programs. At least a second step and possibly a third is necessary before DFD contains enough detail to proceed with programs. During the second step, each procedure of the top-level DFD is taken in isolation and "exploded" into a complete DFD. This is repeated for every procedure. A third step may be required until each procedure is small enough to be written as a short (usually less than 100 lines) stylized program.

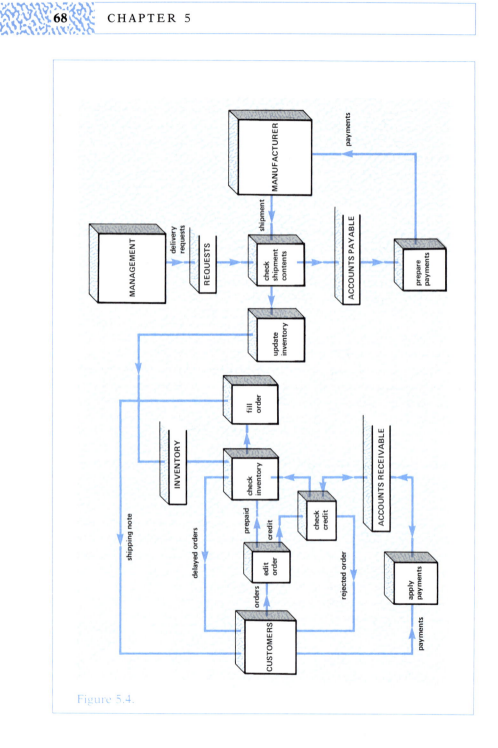

Figure 5.4.

The following DFD (Figure 5.5) shows the explosion of "apply payments" procedure from the previous DFD:

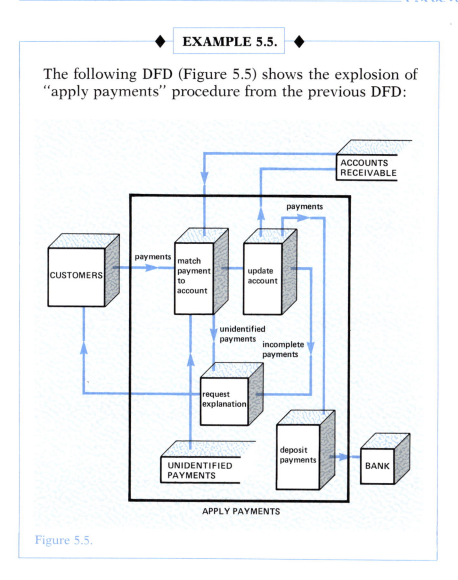

Figure 5.5.

The whole process of explosions creates a multitude of DFDs that have to be linked, stored, and retrieved for analysis. A search for a particular DFD, or worse yet DFDs involving a particular procedure, flow, or file is a complicated search task, and computer aid in this task is generally welcome. Computer aided systems analysis and computer aided software engineering are popular fields of study and many commercial software packages are available for this purpose. Excelerator of Index Technology of Boston, MA and Business Systems Planning (BSP) of IBM are the most popular computer aided techniques.

## *System Specification*

A second group of systems analysis techniques depends on the specification of procedures directly rather than the data flows among them. The best example of this group is the Jackson System Development (JSD) method. This method is based on classifying procedures according to the agents that are involved in the procedure, and time sequencing of procedures within each class. This approach is effective in capturing a great deal of semantics with a minimal number of constructs.

The major constructs of JSD are entities and actions. An *entity* is a thing about which we collect information, and an *action* is an event that affects the information about that entity. Entities and actions are real-world concepts. They are not part of the information system, but part of the organization served by the system. The entities may perform actions, or they may suffer the consequences of actions performed by other entities. JSD starts by listing all entities and their actions, whether performed or suffered.

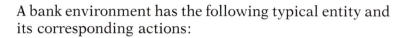

## EXAMPLE 5.6.

A bank environment has the following typical entity and its corresponding actions:

ENTITY       ACTIONS

customer  open account, close account, deposit, withdraw, receive interest, complain, apply for loan, receive loan, pay interest

It is important to note that actions take place at a point in time, rather than extending over a period of time. They are not descriptions of entities such as the customer's address or his account balance. Those would be better characterized as data. *Actions* are events that take place and influence the description of entities. Those familiar with systems science will recognize data as capturing the state of the system, and actions as capturing the events. The *state* of a system describes the system at a given point in time, and *events* are the changes that take place in the state of a system. For example, a customer's address is part of the state of the system (i.e., data) but his moving and the resulting change of address is an event (i.e., action). JSD deals only with entities and their actions. A similar technique dealing with entities and their data will be studied as database design in Chapter 10.

The next stage of JSD is the time sequencing of actions. An entity does not take actions in an arbitrary sequence, and the required sequence contains a great deal of semantic information about the procedures. JSD expresses the required sequence of actions diagrammatically, including some notation to indicate repeated actions and alternative actions.

The following diagram shows the actions of a customer in a bank environment where each customer is required to open an account, perform some transactions, and then close the account, in that order. Each transaction in turn may be a deposit or a withdrawal (Figure 5.6):

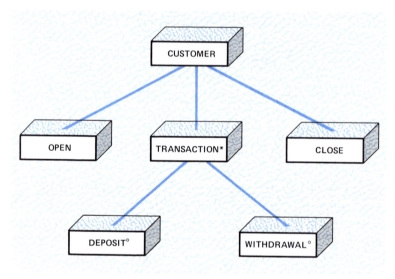

Figure 5.6.

The * implies repetition of an action 0, 1, or more times; and o implies alternative actions.

This model of a bank customer has the major shortcoming of not allowing multiple accounts for a customer. It doesn't even allow a customer to come back to open another account after closing one, except by treating him as a completely new customer. This model requires each customer to open an account, to perform transactions, and to close an account and exit the system. In general, a bank customer would mix opening, closing, and transaction actions in an arbitrary order, and deal with multiple accounts.

The following JSD diagrams allow customers to deal with multiple accounts while enforcing them to open, perform transactions, and close each account in that order. It is important to prevent customers from closing accounts they have not opened, or performing transactions on nonexisting accounts (Figure 5.7):

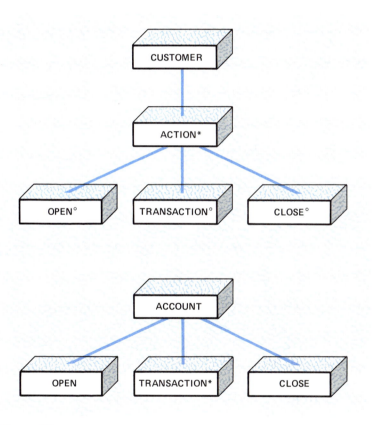

Figure 5.7.

Note that each action appears twice, since an entity takes the action, and another entity suffers it. Each action has to fit into both sequences, which prevents an account being closed before it is opened or opened twice

**EXAMPLE 5.8.** (*Continued*)

because of the ACCOUNT sequence, while allowing the customer to have an arbitrary sequence of actions. The shortcoming of this model is that it does not link each account to a customer. Consequently, there is nothing to prevent a customer from closing somebody else's account or, worse yet, withdrawing from it.

◆ **EXAMPLE 5.9.** ◆

The following JSD diagram links the CUSTOMER and ACCOUNT entities by creating an artificial entity corresponding to each pair (Figure 5.8):

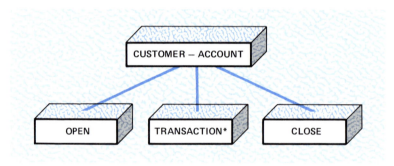

Figure 5.8.

This model allows a customer to have multiple accounts by treating each pair as a separate entity. It restricts the customer to follow the OPEN-TRANSACT-CLOSE sequence for each account, and it prevents a customer from meddling in somebody else's account, since only valid CUSTOMER-ACCOUNT pairs are in the system and each pair is restricted to the given sequence of actions. This is a correct model of the bank customer's behavior. The entities CUSTOMER and ACCOUNT may or may not appear separately as JSD diagrams depending on whether or not they have an independent existence, and whether or not they have other actions to perform.

A complete JSD diagram for a distribution environment with inventory is shown below (Figure 5.9):

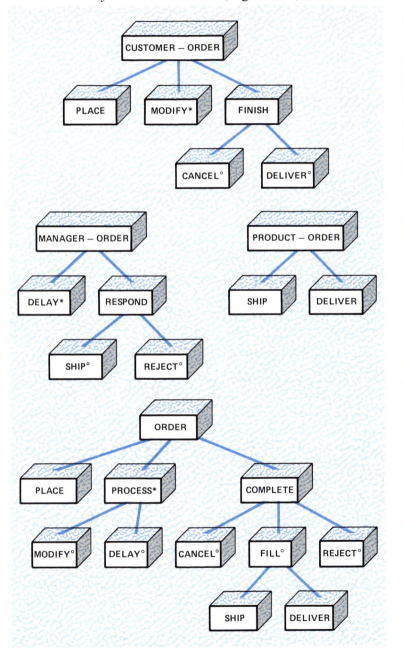

Figure 5.9.

**EXAMPLE 5.10.** (*Continued*)

| ENTITY | ACTIONS |
|--------|---------|
| customer | place, modify, cancel, deliver |
| manager | delay, ship, reject |
| order | place, modify, cancel, deliver, delay, ship, reject |
| product | ship, deliver |

where customers may place orders, modify, or cancel them or receive deliveries; managers may delay an order or ship the products ordered; an order suffers all the actions of customers and managers; and a product may be shipped and consequently delivered to a customer.

The other JSD diagrams corresponding to CUSTOMER, MANAGER, and PRODUCT do not impose any new restrictions on the actions and they will not be included in the specification. Note that the JSD for ORDER is necessary, since otherwise it would be possible for a manager to delay an order that has not been placed, or fill a cancelled order by shipping the products.

The complete specification contains a JSD diagram corresponding to each entity, listing all of its actions, and showing its time relationships. There are additional JSD diagrams corresponding to some pairs of entities and even some triplets. For a pair of entities to have a JSD diagram, first of all they have to have some common actions. Moreover, there must be some restrictions on the actions that cannot be expressed by individual entity JSD diagrams. These situations arise when entities of a given type cannot substitute for each other, and a pair has to perform a given sequence of actions. A typical example above is that a customer cannot cancel another customer's order or modify it. Consequently, a JSD diagram corresponding to CUSTOMER-ORDER pair is necessary. Once a JSD diagram for a pair is drawn, it is necessary to consider the elimination of the individual entity JSD diagrams. The CUSTOMER-ORDER diagram above contains all the information of CUSTOMER, both in terms of the list of actions and the restrictions, and hence the CUSTOMER JSD diagram can be eliminated.

JSD diagrams have a sound theoretical foundation based on systems science and they are easier to draw and analyze than DFDs. However, they are not as popular since they do not capture as much detail and may not be adequate for direct implementation. Similar specification models include PSL/PSA of University of Michigan, and Warnier diagrams.

## Systems Analysis Case

### Distribution with Inventory

Ace Widget Company is a catalog order widget company with an inventory of approximately 200 different widgets. The widgets can be ordered by retail stores from a 25-page merchandise catalog which includes order forms. All inventory is stored in a single central warehouse in Chicago. It is a large five-story, 10,000 square-foot building with a high level of automation in moving inventory items within the building.

The information system, on the other hand, is totally manual, involving separate ledger cards for each catalog item. The ledger cards are maintained by the accounting department. Any changes in the stock status caused by orders, receipt of goods, shipments, or backorders are entered on the appropriate ledger card. At the end of the month all transactions are totaled and the new balances of stock are determined. The new balances are entered on new ledger cards at the beginning of each month. Once a year a physical count of inventory is taken and compared to the amounts on ledger cards. Often significant differences are found between the two amounts with no obvious reason. These are attributed to recording errors and written off.

There is a purchasing agent for each of 24 product lines. She is the person who determines order quantities, dates, and suppliers, and writes purchase orders. Purchase order blanks are standardized and numbered. Copies of each purchase order are sent to accounting for posting on ledger cards, to the receiving department, to the vendor, and to the buyer. The buyer has to be informed about pending orders so that he can use that information to decide reorder points and quantities.

Processing orders from retailers is also done manually. Once a month retailers send in standard order forms with a page for each item ordered, indicating item number, quantity, and possible substitute items acceptable if the actual item is unavailable. When the orders are received by Ace, the credit manager checks the credit status of the retailer and approves or rejects the order. Once the credit is approved, the order form is sent to the shipping clerk where it is filled from inventory. A copy of the order form is enclosed with the shipment as a packing slip.

One copy of the order form is always sent to the accounting department where it is extended and totaled. An invoice is prepared to update accounts receivable and a copy is sent to the retailer. Payments to accounts are also sent to the accounting department for posting. Summary statements are prepared for management on a quarterly basis.

Accounts payable are based on purchase orders, vendors' packing lists, and the vendor invoices. Accounting department keeps the original purchase orders and the vendors' packing lists, and uses them to verify vendors' invoices. Any discrepancy is reported back to the vendor and to the management. Approved invoices are held until due date and then a check is mailed. For vendors with discount policies for early payment, management makes a payment policy decision and the policy is followed. The payment policy for each vendor is recorded in a handbook of payment policies.

## QUESTIONS

1. Draw a DFD describing the information flow in an organization with which you are familiar.

2. Explode one procedure into a second-level DFD.

3. Pick one procedure in the second-level DFD and program it.

4. Draw JSD diagrams for the same organization.

5. Program one of the procedures in your JSD diagram.

6. Repeat the first five questions for the company in Systems Analysis Case section.

7. Revise Example 5.9 so that customers cannot cancel after a modification.

## BIBLIOGRAPHY

Amadio, W. *Systems Development.* Santa Cruz, CA: Mitchell Publishing, Inc., 1989.

Couger, J. D., Colter, M. A., Knapp, R. W. *Advanced System Development/Feasibility Techniques.* New York: John Wiley & Sons, 1982.

Jackson, M. *System Development.* Englewood Cliffs, NJ: Prentice-Hall, 1983.

Wetherbe, J. C. *Systems Analysis and Design.* St. Paul, MN: West Publishing Co., 1984.

# *Part*
# *II*

◆

# *Database Application Systems*

A database application system involves a shared reservoir of data, called a *database*, and a collection of programs each interacting with the database. All applications in this environment share the same database, and the database is managed as a shared resource by a software system called the "database management system." The manager in charge of this shared resource is called a "database administrator." The major advantage of a database environment is the sharing it facilitates, and the consequent minimization of redundancy. In an environment where many applications are based on the same common data, a central database may lead to significant cost savings. This environment is typical of management reporting where many applications serving the reporting needs of different functional areas such as marketing, finance, and operations, and the reporting needs of different managerial levels such as operational, tactical, and strategic management are all based on the same operational data. For this reason, most management reporting systems, called "management information systems," are designed around central databases and fall into the category of database application systems. The major disadvantage of database application systems is the overhead associated with maintaining a central utility. The most critical component of the overhead is the cost of maintaining a structure that serves the needs of all users, without undue bias toward any particular user. The accessibility of the data to all who need it, and in a form they need it, is a difficult technical problem since users and their needs are diverse. The technical difficulty of the problem creates an intense political battle among users to direct the limited funds of the database administrator to serve their particular data needs. The office of the database administrator is a highly political office that involves reconciling the variety of user needs into one structure that serves most of them satisfactorily. The second component of the overhead is the difficulty of locating and retrieving the relevant data for each user from a large shared pool. This task is considerably more difficult and costly than using a custom-designed system serving only one application. The transition from a data processing environment to a database environment is justified when there is sufficient overlap among data needs of applications so that the benefits from elimination of redundancy exceed the cost of overhead resulting from centralized management.

# *Chapter 6*

◆

# Databases

A *database* is a collection of interrelated files. It is a large shared resource and it has to be structured to respond to the needs of a variety of users efficiently. Moreover, the set of users and their needs constantly change, and the database is expected to continue to meet such dynamic requirements without costly major development or restructuring. The structures necessary to meet changing requirements of a variety of users are complex and difficult to build and use. Consequently, the database philosophy faces a major compromise between two conflicting objectives. The objective of building a system that can be all things to all users conflicts with the simplicity and ease of use. Both objectives are important, and instead of sacrificing one objective for the sake of the other, modern database management systems attempt to provide both through elaborate mechanisms. Modern database philosophy can be summarized, then, as the development of techniques to provide both generality and simplicity within one system. The two objectives are

1. to build a system that can respond to as many requests as possible, foreseeable or unforeseen at the time of design.

2. to hide as much irrelevant information as possible from each user, making it appear personalized to simplify the use of the system.

The major tool to meet these objectives is *abstraction*. Complex structures that are necessary to make the system more general can be hidden from some users through multiple levels of abstraction. Each level of abstraction may be appropriate for a different type of user and contains only the information that type of user needs. Typically, three levels of abstraction are employed by modern database management systems.

1. *Physical structure* is also called *internal structure*. It deals with the actual placement of data items on the storage device, and the actual implementation of access paths linking a data item to others. All the index files, pointers, and search strategies are visible to the user. The structures discussed in previous chapters are all physical structures. A user of physical structures has to navigate in a sea of data to locate his own data by following the access paths. The major task of the user as a navigator is to find the best path to reach a particular data item. As discussed in Part I, optimization is a major activity of a user of physical structures.

2. *Logical structure* is also called *conceptual structure* or *schema*. It provides an abstract structure showing a description of data in the system, and their relationships. Logical structures are often described as subway maps that tell you what items are connected but not all the details of how they are connected. Like a subway map that hides all the information about bridges, tunnels, and distances, a logical structure hides all the information about pointers, index files, overflow areas, and search strategies.

3. *External structure* is also called a *subschema* or a *user view*. It is merely a subset of the logical structure. It contains only a portion of the logical structure relevant to a particular user. It is similar to a partial map, showing only a particular subway route designed for the users of that route.

Most users of databases see only logical structures, and all their activities are guided by the logical structures. There are many types of logical structures, each appropriate for a different kind of environment. The general categories of logical structures are called *data models,* and the two major data models, *network* and *relational* models, will be studied in detail in Chapters 7 and 8. *Data models* are characterized by the assumptions they make about the application environment, and the amount of physical detail they hide from the users. Obviously, the more stringent the assumptions are, the less general is the resulting model, but the easier it is to implement. Generality versus efficiency is a major tradeoff in data models. Every major assumption about the environment allows a better optimization of the underlying physical structure, utilizing the information provided by the assumption, but increases the risk that at some point during the lifetime of the system its basic assumptions will be violated, rendering the system useless, at least for that application.

◆  **EXAMPLE 6.1.**  ◆

A phone book designed to respond only to questions requesting the phone number given the name of the customer will be useless if a phone number is given and the name is requested.

Data models are also differentiated with respect to the amount of information they hide. All data models hide a great deal of physical detail from users, and every detail that is hidden from the users increases the responsibility taken by the system, since what is not seen by the user has to be created and maintained by the system. The more abstract a data model gets by hiding information the easier it is to use the system, and the more difficult it is for the system to create efficient structures and maintain their efficiency. High-level data models require a great deal of optimization to be done by the system automatically. The optimization procedures are complex, and costly to develop and execute. Efficiency usually is the difference between a \$20K and \$200K database management system.

Every data model comes with two languages to allow the manipulation and access to the data it represents. Data definition language (DDL) is used to define the logical structure of a database. Data manipulation language (DML) is used to load, update, and retrieve the actual data. DDLs are usually straightforward. They contain a creation command for every component of the structure they support. DMLs are complex and varied, and they will occupy most of our attention in the next two chapters.

## QUESTIONS

1. What is a database? What is the database philosophy?

2. Explain the objectives of the three levels of abstraction employed by modern database management systems.

3. What is a data model?

## BIBLIOGRAPHY

Kroenke, D., Dolan, K. *Database Processing.* Chicago: Science Research Associates, 1985.

Tsichritzis, D. C., Lochovsky, F. H. *Data Models.* Englewood Cliffs, NJ: Prentice-Hall, 1982.

◆

# Chapter 7

# Network Model

A *network structure* contains the names of files and their attributes, the names of the key and the secondary key attributes,
and the names and the nature of relationships among files.

◆ **EXAMPLE 7.1.** ◆

A typical network structure corresponding to the physical structure given in Example 3.7 is shown below.

PS ⟶ PART (<u>number</u>, type, $\overline{\text{price}}$)
⟶ SUPPLIER (<u>number</u>, credit-limit)

The information contained in this structure is the following: Two files are given. The PART file contains three
attributes: number, type, and price. Number is the key
attribute; price is a secondary key. Similarly, the
SUPPLIER file contains two attributes: number and
credit-limit, and number is the key. There is a many-to-
many relationship named **PS** between the two files.
Double arrows indicate a many-to-many relationship. A
single arrow on one side would mean a many-to-one
relationship, with the single arrow on the one side. Two

**EXAMPLE 7.1.** (*Continued*)

single arrows would be used to denote a one-to-one relationship.

The information that is hidden by this structure is as important as the information revealed. The structure does not reveal the file structure, whether it is contiguous or dispersed, and whether it is sorted or not. It does not reveal the search strategy whether it is sequential, blocked, or binary. It does not show the maintenance strategy, and the associated structures such as overflow files and overflow pointers. The physical structure associated with the secondary keys such as index files and chains is not shown, nor is the implementation details of the relationship such as intersection files and rings. The system takes responsibility for the efficiency of all hidden structures including optimum block sizes, and optimum timing of reorganization, as discussed in Chapter 2.

## *Types of Networks*

There are three general types of networks, characterized by the types of relationships they allow. The most restrictive type of network is a *hierarchy*. A hierarchical structure does not allow many-to-many relationships but only one-to-one and many-to-one relationships. Moreover, each file in a hierarchical structure has no more than one parent file (see Example 7.2).

Some popular commercial hierarchical database management systems are IMS and DL/I of IBM, and System 2000 of MRI Corporation.

Simple networks are less restrictive than hierarchies. They still do not allow many-to-many relationships, but they impose no restrictions regarding the number of parents each file can have (see Example 7.3).

---

◆ **EXAMPLE 7.2.** ◆

A typical hierarchical structure is shown below.

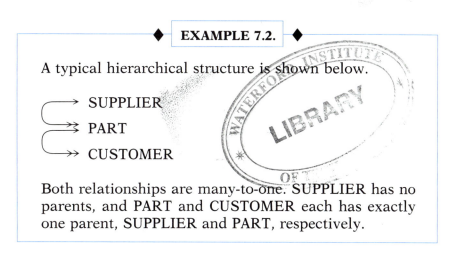

Both relationships are many-to-one. SUPPLIER has no parents, and PART and CUSTOMER each has exactly one parent, SUPPLIER and PART, respectively.

---

◆ **EXAMPLE 7.3.** ◆

A typical simple network structure is shown below.

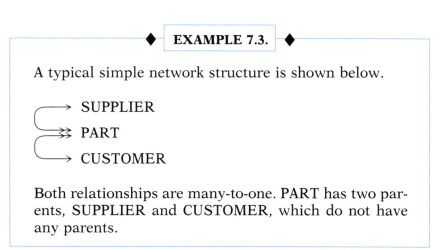

Both relationships are many-to-one. PART has two parents, SUPPLIER and CUSTOMER, which do not have any parents.

---

Complex networks are the most general network structures. They allow many-to-many relationships, and impose no other restrictions (see Example 7.4, page 90).

The distinction among the types of networks is important for implementation purposes. Obviously, more restrictive models are easier to implement, but are more likely to become difficult to use when their assumptions are violated. A hierarchical structure can be implemented with at most two rings

◆ **EXAMPLE 7.4.** ◆

A typical complex network structure is shown below.

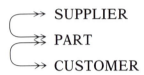
SUPPLIER

PART

CUSTOMER

Some popular commercial simple and complex network database management systems are TOTAL of Cincom Corporation, IDS of Honeywell, and IDMS of IBM.

going through each record; one linking it to its parent, another to its children. All children of a parent record are linked together in one giant ring passing through multiple files. Simple networks are more difficult to implement. They require multiple rings through each record, each corresponding to a different parent. The number of rings per record is the same for all records of a file although it may vary from file to file depending on how many parents a file has. However, since the number of parents of a file is fixed at the design phase, and hence the number of pointers per record is fixed for each file, the structure is still easily implementable. Complex networks, on the other hand, require intersection files, as discussed in Chapter 3.

## *Network Languages*

*Network languages* are called record-at-a-time languages, since they retrieve one record at a time for processing. These languages are similar to programming languages in the sense that they provide sequential, conditional, and looping instructions. In addition, they provide two critical commands, FIND and MAP. FIND is used to search a file and locate the records that satisfy a given criteria as discussed in Chapter 2. The FIND command alone accomplishes everything that was discussed in Chapter 2, of course without revealing the physical details of the search. MAP is used to traverse a relationship between two files. It starts with a record in a given file, and finds all records related to that record in the second file. The MAP command alone accomplishes everything that was discussed in Chapter 3, of course without revealing all the physical details of the relationship implementation. In addition to FIND and MAP, a network language contains a number of standard programming language commands such as OPEN, PRINT, LET, IF, and DO FOR as discussed in Chapter 4. These commands maintain the same interpretation as in programming languages. The basic philosophy of a network language is to employ two types of cursors, called *currency indicators,* to indicate which record of which file is currently being processed. The structure is traversed by moving the currency indicators around, using the commands of the language. There are two types of currency indicators. The *current file* indicator points to the file that is currently being processed, and the *current record* indicator in each file points to the record currently being processed in each file. The current record of the current file is the record receiving immediate attention. The first file opened is the current file initially, and the current file indicator can be reset using the SET CURRENT command. The MAP command resets the current file indicator to the destination of the map, and the FOR command resets it at the start of each iteration to the file associated with it. The current record indicator is initially set by the FIND command, a FOR loop resets it to the next record in each iteration, and the MAP command also sets the current record indicator when it moves to a new file. A stylized network language will be demonstrated through a series of examples, given the following network structure:

$$SS \begin{cases} \longrightarrow \text{SUPPLY} \quad (\underline{\text{LNO}}, \overline{\text{PNO}}) \\ \longrightarrow \text{SUPPLIER} \ (\underline{\text{SNO}}, \text{LOC}) \end{cases}$$

Where the SUPPLY file contains supply number (or invoice number) LNO and part number PNO for each shipment; the SUPPLIER file contains the supplier number SNO, and the location LOC of each supplier. The relationship SS identifies the supplier of each shipment.

---

◆ **EXAMPLE 7.5.** ◆

Find supplies of part 1121.

```
OPEN SUPPLY
FIND PNO=1121
FOR EACH SUPPLY
      PRINT LNO
NEXT SUPPLY
```

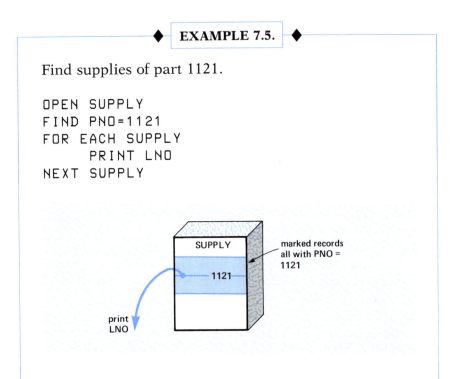

The program opens the SUPPLY file, locates all records satisfying the condition PNO = 1121, and marks those records for transportation to main memory, and the loop retrieves those marked records one at a time and prints their LNO values.

---

◆ **EXAMPLE 7.6.** ◆

Find supplies of a part other than 1121.

```
OPEN SUPPLY
FIND PNO≠1121
FOR EACH SUPPLY
     PRINT LNO
NEXT SUPPLY
```

The program is similar to the previous one except for the use of ≠ as opposed to = .

---

◆ **EXAMPLE 7.7.** ◆

Find supplies of part 1121 or part 1790.

```
OPEN SUPPLY
FIND PNO=1121 OR PNO=1790
FOR EACH SUPPLY
     PRINT LNO
NEXT SUPPLY
```

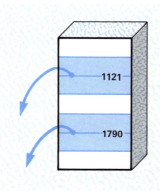

---

**EXAMPLE 7.7.** (*Continued*)

The FIND command can accept multiple conditions connected with logical operations **OR** and **AND**.

---

◆ **EXAMPLE 7.8.** ◆

Find the locations supplying part 1121.

```
OPEN SUPPLY SUPPLIER
FIND PNO=1121
FOR EACH SUPPLY
     MAP TO SUPPLIER VIA SS
     PRINT LOC
NEXT SUPPLY
```

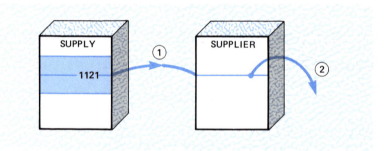

The program demonstrates the MAP command. Two files are opened. The first file listed, SUPPLY, is the current file. All SUPPLY records with PNO = 1121 are located, marked, and the first one is set as the current record. The loop retrieves the marked records one at a time advancing the currency indicator at each step. For each supply record, the MAP command locates the related SUPPLIER record via the relationship SS. It moves the current file indicator to SUPPLIER and the current record indicator in SUPPLIER to the record found. Finally, it prints the LOC value of the supplier found, and repeats the process.

Find the suppliers who supply part 1121 and part 1790.

```
OPEN SUPPLY.1 SUPPLIER SUPPLY.2
FIND PNO=1121
FOR EACH SUPPLY.1
      MAP TO SUPPLIER VIA SS
      MAP TO SUPPLY.2 VIA SS
      FOR EACH SUPPLY.2
            IF PNO=1790
                  MAP TO SUPPLIER VIA SS
                  PRINT SNO
            END
      NEXT SUPPLY.2
NEXT SUPPLY.1
```

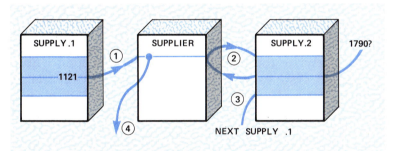

The best way to visualize this program is to assume the existence of two separate copies of the SUPPLY file, SUPPLY.1 and SUPPLY.2. SUPPLY.1 is used to check if 1121 is supplied by a supplier, and SUPPLY.2 is used to check if the same supplier supplies 1790. Conceptually, two copies are necessary since only one loop per file can be executed at a time. In reality, of course, there is only one copy of the file, but two currency indicators are created to execute two simultaneous loops. The program starts with the SUPPLY.1 file by finding all supply records where PNO = 1121. The supplier of each of these records obviously is a supplier of 1121. To test if he also supplies 1790, a MAP to the SUPPLY.2 file is used, and all supplies from this supplier are searched for the part 1790. If 1790 is found then to print the supplier number, one has to map back to the SUPPLIER file since SNO

**EXAMPLE 7.9.** (*Continued*)

is an attribute of the SUPPLIER file. This program can also be written by starting with the SUPPLIER file, and for each supplier record checking two conditions. A map to SUPPLY.1 and a check for the part 1121, and a map to SUPPLY.2 and a check for the part 1790 are the two conditions. If both conditions are satisfied then the supplier is returned. Clearly, this program is not as efficient as the original program. It has to repeat the two checks for every record in the SUPPLIER file, while the original program only considered the suppliers of the part 1121 by using the FIND command initially. In general, programs that process all records in a file are considered inefficient and that prospect should be avoided whenever possible. The user of a network system is responsible for avoiding long file searches since the system cannot rewrite the programs to optimize them. Unlike relational systems, the user of a network system is responsible for the efficiency of the programs to a large extent.

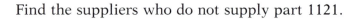

**EXAMPLE 7.10.**

Find the suppliers who do not supply part 1121.

```
OPEN SUPPLIER SUPPLY
FIND ALL
FOR EACH SUPPLIER
     MAP TO SUPPLY VIA SS
     FOR EACH SUPPLY
          IF PNO=1121
               NEXT SUPPLIER
          END
     NEXT SUPPLY
     MAP TO SUPPLIER VIA SS
     PRINT SNO
NEXT SUPPLIER
```

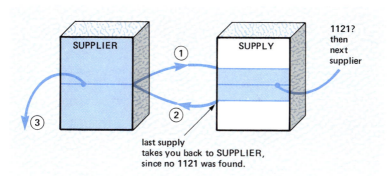

last supply
takes you back to SUPPLIER,
since no 1121 was found.

To formulate a negative question like this one, all supplies of each supplier have to be checked. If none of them is 1121, then a supplier has been found. If any of his supplies is of 1121, then the program moves to the next supplier.

◆ **EXAMPLE 7.11.** ◆

Find the suppliers who supply part 1121 but not part 1790.

```
OPEN SUPPLY.1 SUPPLIER SUPPLY.2
FIND PNO=1121
FOR EACH SUPPLY.1
      MAP TO SUPPLIER VIA SS
      MAP TO SUPPLY.2 VIA SS
      FOR EACH SUPPLY.2
          IF PNO=1790
              NEXT SUPPLY.1
          END
      NEXT SUPPLY.2
      MAP TO SUPPLIER VIA SS
      PRINT SNO
NEXT SUPPLY.1
```

## EXAMPLE 7.11. (*Continued*)

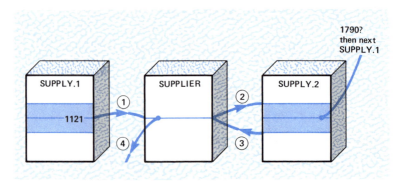

This program is a combination of the two programs given in Examples 7.9 and 7.10.

---

## ◆ EXAMPLE 7.12. ◆

Find the suppliers who supply all parts.

```
OPEN SUPPLIER SUPPLY.1 SUPPLY.2
FIND ALL
FOR EACH SUPPLIER
     SET CURRENT SUPPLY.1
     FIND ALL
     FOR EACH SUPPLY.1
          LET P=PNO
          SET CURRENT SUPPLIER
          MAP TO SUPPLY.2 VIA SS
          FOR EACH SUPPLY.2
             IF PNO=P
                  NEXT SUPPLY.1
             ELSE
                  NEXT SUPPLY.2
             END
          NEXT SUPPLY.2
          NEXT SUPPLIER
     NEXT SUPPLY.1
     SET CURRENT SUPPLIER
     PRINT SNO
NEXT SUPPLIER
```

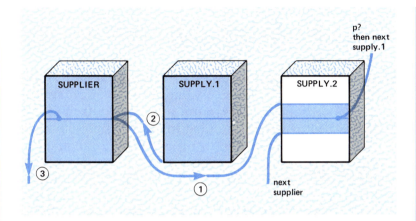

This program demonstrates the LET command to assign a database value to a temporary variable, and the SET CURRENT command to explicitly change the current file indicator. The program uses the SUPPLY.1 file as a list of parts since no separate PART file exists. For a given supplier, the program goes through the complete list of parts in the SUPPLY.1 file, and tests if the supplier supplies each part. If a part is found that he does not supply then the program moves on to the next supplier. If he supplies them all then his SNO is printed. The first loop corresponds to SUPPLIER records, the second loop is for SUPPLY.1, and the third loop is for SUPPLY.2 records. A normal exit from the second loop means for each part listed in SUPPLY.1 file, a record in SUPPLY.2 is found to indicate that this part is supplied by the current supplier, and hence the current supplier is printed as having supplied all parts.

It is important to remember that each FOR loop is associated with a file and each iteration resets that file as the current file. OPEN, MAP, and SET are the other commands that set the current file indicator. The current record indicator is also advanced by each iteration of the FOR loop. FIND and MAP are the other commands that set the current record indicator.

## Network Data Language (NDL)

NDL was designed and adopted by the American National Standards Institute (ANSI) as a standard network language in 1986. Its basic commands are similar to the stylized language of Chapter 7, but it is not intended to be a complete language. It is used in conjunction with a programming language such as COBOL or PASCAL, and NDL commands are issued from within the programming languages. The NDL commands are distinguished from the programming language commands by the prefix "NDL" attached to them. Corresponding to the FIND command of network systems, NDL provides two commands. NDL-FIND FIRST finds the first record in a file, and NDL-FIND NEXT finds the next record by moving the current record pointer. To traverse a file, a loop is needed, and the first record is found outside the loop, and each iteration through the loop finds a new next record. A DB-STATUS variable indicates the end of the file by containing a value other than 0. The value 0 corresponds to successful retrieval of the next record. Nonzero values each correspond to a different type of error. NDL also provides the additional command NDL-GET since finding a record merely marks it for retrieval and an NDL-GET command is necessary to retrieve it. The MAP command of network systems also corresponds to two commands in NDL. NDL-FIND OWNER is used to map from a child file to the parent file. NDL-FIND IN is used to map from a parent file to a child file. The following substitutions are used to translate from the stylized network language to NDL embedded in a programming language:

| | |
|---|---|
| OPEN SUPPLY | NDL-FIND FIRST SUPPLY |
| FIND PNO = 1121 | WHERE PNO = 1121 |
| | |
| FOR EACH SUPPLY | DO UNTIL DB. STATUS≠0 |
| ≡ | ≡ |
| | |
| NEXT SUPPLY | NDL-FIND NEXT SUPPLY |
| | END |

| | |
|---|---|
| PRINT LNO | NDL-GET SUPPLY SET A TO LNO<br>PRINT A |
| MAP TO SUPPLIER VIA SS | NDL-FIND OWNER SS |
| MAP TO SUPPLY VIA SS | NDL-FIND FIRST SUPPLY IN SS |
| IF PNO = 1790<br>$\equiv$<br>END | NDL-GET SUPPLY SET A TO PNO<br>IF A = 1790<br>$\equiv$<br>END |
| MAP TO SUPPLY.2 VIA SS | NDL-CONNECT SUPPLY TO<br>    SUPPLYLIST<br>NDL-FIND FIRST SUPPLY IN SS<br>$\equiv$<br>NDL-FIND LAST SUPPLY IN<br>    SUPPLYLIST |

The following examples demonstrate NDL as embedded into a stylized programming language, given the network database of the previous section.

◆ **EXAMPLE 7.13.** ◆

Find supplies of part 1121.

```
NDL-FIND FIRST SUPPLY WHERE PNO=1121
DO UNTIL DB.STATUS≠0
 NDL-GET SUPPLY SET A TO LNO
 PRINT A
 NDL-FIND NEXT SUPPLY WHERE PNO=1121
END
```

The program opens the supply file, locates the first record satisfying the condition PNO = 1121 and marks it for transportation to main memory. The loop retrieves the marked record, stores its LNO field in variable A and prints it. The loop gets the next supply record where PNO = 1121, and continues until it fails to find a next record.

---

◆ **EXAMPLE 7.14.** ◆

Find supplies of a part other than 1121.

```
NDL-FIND FIRST SUPPLY WHERE PNO≠1121
DO UNTIL DB.STATUS≠0
 NDL-GET SUPPLY SET A TO LNO
 PRINT A
 NDL-FIND NEXT SUPPLY WHERE PNO≠1121
END
```

The program is similar to the previous one except for the use of ≠ as opposed to =.

---

◆ **EXAMPLE 7.15.** ◆

Find supplies of part 1121 or part 1790.

```
OPEN SUPPLY
NDL-FIND FIRST SUPPLY WHERE PNO=1121
                            OR PNO=1790
DO UNTIL DB-STATUS≠0
 NDL-GET SUPPLY SET A TO LNO
 PRINT A
 NDL-FIND NEXT SUPPLY WHERE PNO=1121
                            OR PNO=1790
END
```

The FIND command can accept multiple conditions connected with logical operations AND and OR.

---

◆ **EXAMPLE 7.16.** ◆

Find the locations supplying part 1121.

```
OPEN SUPPLY SUPPLIER
NDL-FIND FIRST SUPPLY WHERE PNO=1121
DO UNTIL DB-STATUS≠0
 NDL-FIND OWNER SS
 NDL-GET SUPPLIER SET A TO LOC
 PRINT LOC
 NDL-FIND NEXT SUPPLY WHERE PNO=1121
END
```

The program demonstrates mapping between files. Two files are opened. The first supply record with PNO = 1121 is located and marked. The loop continues to find supply records with PNO = 1121 until no more can be found. For each record found FIND OWNER ·command locates the corresponding supplier through the relationship SS, retrieves it, and prints its LOC field.

◆ **EXAMPLE 7.17.** ◆

Find the suppliers who supply part 1121 and part 1790.

```
OPEN SUPPLY SUPPLIER
NDL-FIND FIRST SUPPLY WHERE PNO=1121
DO UNTIL DB-STATUS≠0
 NDL-CONNECT SUPPLY TO SUPPLYLIST
 NDL-FIND OWNER SS
 NDL-FIND FIRST SUPPLY IN SS WHERE PNO=1790
 IF DB-STATUS=0
  NDL-GET SUPPLIER SET A TO SNO
  PRINT A
 END
 NDL-FIND LAST SUPPLY IN SUPPLYLIST
 NDL-FIND NEXT SUPPLY WHERE PNO=1121
END
```

**EXAMPLE 7.17.** (*Continued*)

The program demonstrates two simultaneous searches through the SUPPLY file without creating two copies of the file. The two searches are possible by saving the current record of one search temporarily before moving into the second search, and retrieving the saved record to return to the first search. The program opens two files, finds the first supply where PNO = 1121, and continues to get the next record until no more can be found. For each record found, the program has to find its supplier and check if it also supplied part 1790. This requires a second search in the supply file destroying the currency indicator of the first search. To preserve the currency indicator, the current record of the first search is stored in a SUPPLYLIST and it is retrieved back just before returning to the original search. Within the loop, the supplier of the current supply is found, and within the supplies of this supplier a supply of part 1790 is searched. If found, the supplier is retrieved and its SNO is printed. This program can also be written by starting with the SUPPLIER file and searching for two member records. First finding a supply of 1121 within the relationship SS, and if found then finding a supply of 1790 within the same relationship SS connected to the same supplier. Clearly, this program is not as efficient as the original program. It has to repeat the two checks for every record in the supplier file, while the original program only considers the suppliers of part 1121. In general, the programs that process all records in a file are considered inefficient, and that prospect should be avoided whenever possible.

◆ **EXAMPLE 7.18.** ◆

Find the suppliers who do not supply part 1121.

```
OPEN SUPPLIER SUPPLY
NDL-FIND FIRST SUPPLIER
DO UNTIL DB-STATUS≠0
 NDL-FIND FIRST SUPPLY IN SS WHERE PNO=1121
 IF DBSTATUS≠0
  NDL-GET SUPPLIER SET A TO SNO
  PRINT A
 END
 NDL-FIND NEXT SUPPLIER
END
```

NDL programs can formulate negative questions very concisely by checking if a target set is empty. If DBSTATUS≠0 then no supplier with SNO=1121 has been found and the supplier can be printed to have not supplied part 1121.

◆ **EXAMPLE 7.19.** ◆

Find the suppliers who supply part 1121 but not part 1790.

```
OPEN SUPPLY SUPPLIER
NDL-FIND FIRST SUPPLY WHERE PNO=1121
DO UNTIL DB-STATUS≠0
 NDL-CONNECT SUPPLY TO SUPPLYLIST
 NDL-FIND OWNER SS
 NDL-FIND FIRST SUPPLY IN SS WHERE PNO=1790
 IF DB-STATUS≠0
  NDL-GET SUPPLIER SET A TO SNO
  PRINT A
 END
 NDL-FIND LAST SUPPLY IN SUPPLYLIST
 NDL-FIND NEXT SUPPLY WHERE PNO=1121
END
```

This program is a combination of the last two programs.

♦ ┤ **EXAMPLE 7.20.** ├ ♦

Find the suppliers who supply all parts.

```
OPEN SUPPLY SUPPLIER
NDL-FIND FIRST SUPPLIER
DO UNTIL DB-STATUS≠0
 NDL-FIND FIRST SUPPLY
 DO
  DO UNTIL DB-STATUS≠0
   NDL-CONNECT SUPPLY TO SUPPLYLIST
   NDL-GET SUPPLY SET P TO PNO
   NDL-FIND FIRST SUPPLY IN SS WHERE PNO=P
   IF DB-STATUS≠0
    EXIT
    EXIT
    EXIT
   END
   NDL-FIND LAST SUPPLY IN SUPPLYLIST
   NDL-FIND NEXT SUPPLY
  END
  NDL-GET SUPPLIER SET S TO SNO
  PRINT S
 END
 NDL-FIND NEXT SUPPLIER
END
```

The program uses the SUPPLY file both as a list of supplies and as a list of parts. For a given supplier, the program goes through the complete list of parts in the SUPPLY file, and tests if the supplier supplies each part. If a part is found that he does not supply, then the program moves on to the next supplier. If he supplies them all then his SNO is printed. The first loop corresponds to SUPPLIER records, the second loop is for parts, and the third loop is for supplies. A normal exit from the second loop means that for each part listed in SUPPLY file, there is a record in SUPPLY file indicating that this

> part is supplied by the current supplier, and hence the current supplier is printed as having supplied all the parts.

## *System 1032 Data Programming Language (DPL)*

System 1032 is a network-type system available on Digital Equipment Corporation (DEC) computers. It was developed and marketed by Software House in Massachusetts. It is remarkably similar to the stylized language except that it does not have a complete block structure and some branching is necessary in conjunction with if statements. It does provide block-structured looping, but not block-structured conditionals, consequently the following substitution is required where L1 is a label identifying a line:

```
IF  PNO=1121                   IF  PNO=1121  THEN
    ≡                              ≡
    EXIT                              GOTO  L1
END                            END_IF
                               L1:
```

Also, multiple copies of files cannot be opened, hence the currency indicator must be stored and retrieved to do multiple searches on a file. **SAVE SELECTION_SET** and **RESTORE SELECTION_SET** commands accomplish that task. The substitution is

```
MAP  TO  SUPPLY.2  VIS  SS   SAVE  SELECTION_SET
    ≡                        MAP  TO  SUPPLY  VIA  SS
                                 ≡
                             RESTORE  SELECTION_SET
```

Finally, the name of the file **SUPPLIER** is changed to **SUPPLR** since there is a six-character limit on variable names in DPL.

The following examples demonstrate DPL given the network database of Chapter 7:

---

**EXAMPLE 7.21.**

Find supplies of part 1121.

```
OPEN DATASET SUPPLY
FIND PNO EQ 1121
FOR EACH RECORD DO
    PRINT LNO
END_FOR
```

---

**EXAMPLE 7.22.**

Find supplies of a part other than 1121.

```
OPEN DATASET SUPPLY
FIND PNO NE 1121
FOR EACH RECORD DO
    PRINT LNO
END_FOR
```

---

**EXAMPLE 7.23.**

Find supplies of part 1121 or part 1790.

```
OPEN DATASET SUPPLY
FIND PNO EQ 1121 OR PNO EQ 1790
FOR EACH RECORD DO
    PRINT LNO
END_FOR
```

---

**♦ EXAMPLE 7.24. ♦**

Find the locations supplying part 1121.

```
OPEN DATASET SUPPLY SUPPLR
FIND PNO EQ 1121
FOR EACH RECORD DO
    MAP TO SUPPLR VIA SS
    PRINT LOC
END_FOR
```

---

**♦ EXAMPLE 7.25. ♦**

Find the suppliers who supply part 1121 and part 1790.

```
OPEN DATASET SUPPLY SUPPLR
FIND PNO EQ 1121
FOR EACH RECORD DO
    SAVE SELECTION_SET
    MAP TO SUPPLR VIA SS
    MAP TO SUPPLY VIA SS
    FOR EACH RECORD DO
        IF PNO EQ 1790 THEN
            SET DATASET SUPPLR
            PRINT SNO
            GOTO L1
        END_IF
    END_FOR
    L1: SET DATASET SUPPLY
    RESTORE SELECTION_SET
END_FOR
```

EXAMPLE 7.26.

Find the suppliers who do not supply part 1121.

```
OPEN DATASET SUPPLR SUPPLY
FIND ALL
FOR EACH RECORD DO
    MAP TO SUPPLY VIA SS
    FOR EACH RECORD DO
        IF PNO EQ 1121 THEN
            GOTO L1
        END_IF
    END_FOR
    SET DATASET SUPPLR
    PRINT SNO
L1:END_FOR
```

EXAMPLE 7.27.

Find the suppliers who supply part 1121 but not part 1790.

```
OPEN DATASET SUPPLY SUPPLR
FIND PNO EQ 1121
FOR EACH RECORD DO
    SAVE SELECTION_SET
    MAP TO SUPPLR VIA SS
    MAP TO SUPPLY VIA SS
    FOR EACH RECORD DO
        IF PNO EQ 1790 THEN
            GOTO L1
        END_IF
    END_FOR
    SET DATASET SUPPLR
    PRINT SNO
    L1:SET DATASET SUPPLY
    RESTORE SELECTION_SET
END_FOR
```

◆ **EXAMPLE 7.28.** ◆

Find the suppliers who supplied all parts.

```
VARIABLE B INTEGER
OPEN DATASET SUPPLR SUPPLY
FIND ALL
FOR EACH RECORD DO
     SET DATASET SUPPLY
     FIND ALL
     FOR EACH RECORD DO
          SAVE SELECTION_SET
          LET B=PNO
          SET DATASET SUPPLR
          MAP TO SUPPLY VIA SS
          FOR EACH RECORD DO
               IF PNO EQ B THEN
                    GOTO L1
               END_IF
          END_FOR
          GOTO L2
          L1:RESTORE SELECTION_SET
     END_FOR
     SET DATASET SUPPLR
     PRINT SNO
L2:SET DATASET SUPPLR
END_FOR
```

## QUESTIONS

1. Characterize the following database structure as to its type:

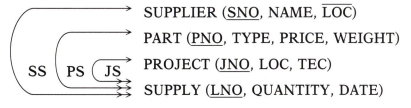

SUPPLIER (<u>SNO</u>, NAME, $\overline{\text{LOC}}$)

PART (<u>PNO</u>, TYPE, PRICE, WEIGHT)

PROJECT (<u>JNO</u>, LOC, TEC)

SUPPLY (<u>LNO</u>, QUANTITY, DATE)

where **SUPPLIER** contains the supplier number, name and location of each supplier; **PART** contains part number, type, price, and weight of each existing part; **PROJECT** contains the project number, location, and the total estimated cost of all projects in this enterprise; and **SUPPLY** contains the supply invoice number, quantity supplied, and the date of receipt for each shipment. Each shipment of supplies is linked to its supplier through **SS**, to the part contained in the shipment through **PS**, and to the project receiving the supply through **JS**.

2. Locate a network database management system available at your computer system and ask your database administrator to define the data structure of Question 1 and load the following data:

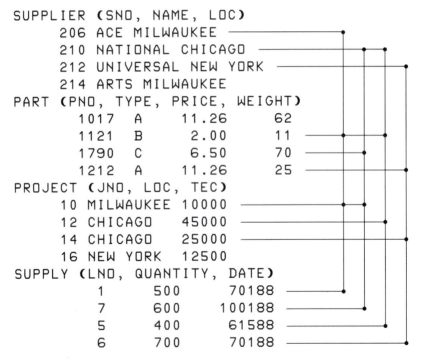

```
SUPPLIER (SNO, NAME, LOC)
      206 ACE MILWAUKEE
      210 NATIONAL CHICAGO
      212 UNIVERSAL NEW YORK
      214 ARTS MILWAUKEE
PART (PNO, TYPE, PRICE, WEIGHT)
      1017   A     11.26      62
      1121   B      2.00      11
      1790   C      6.50      70
      1212   A     11.26      25
PROJECT (JNO, LOC, TEC)
      10 MILWAUKEE 10000
      12 CHICAGO    45000
      14 CHICAGO    25000
      16 NEW YORK   12500
SUPPLY (LNO, QUANTITY, DATE)
      1        500      70188
      7        600     100188
      5        400      61588
      6        700      70188
```

3. Write programs using the stylized network language introduced in this chapter to pose the following questions:

a. Suppliers in Chicago
b. Parts supplied by supplier 210
c. Parts supplied by a supplier other than 210
d. Parts supplied by 210 or 206
e. Parts supplied by 210 and 206
f. Parts supplied from Chicago
g. Parts supplied from Chicago to Chicago
h. Part types supplied
i. Parts not supplied to project 14
j. Parts not supplied
k. Parts of type A supplied by supplier 212 to project 14
l. Parts supplied to all projects

4. Learn the DML of your network system and compare it to the stylized network language introduced in this chapter. Identify all differences.

5. Write programs using the DML of your system to pose the questions a through l listed above. Debug and execute your programs.

6. Try to collect evidence for the correctness of your programs. For example, make sure the answer to g is a subset of the answer to f, and e is a subset of b. Can the answers to b and c have any common elements? How about the answers to i and l?

# BIBLIOGRAPHY

Bradley, J. *File and Database Techniques.* New York: Holt, Rinehart and Winston, 1982.

Cardenas, A. F. *Database Management Systems.* Needham Hts, MA: Allyn & Bacon Inc., 1979.

# Chapter 8

♦

# Relational Model

The relational model of data has three general objectives.

1. Further simplification of logical structures by eliminating more of the physical details such as secondary keys and relationships.
2. Simplification of the data languages by dealing with sets of data at a time, as opposed to record-at-a-time logic. This strategy leads to the elimination of all looping and branching from the data languages, producing algebra- or logic-based languages.
3. General-purpose implementations where all questions can be answered as efficiently as possible without burdening the user with the optimization. This objective requires rewriting of the programs by the system to reflect the optimum retrieval strategies developed by the system. Such extensive optimization by the system relieves the user from much of the programming effort.

A typical relational structure is given below for the manufacturing environment of Chapter 7.

> SUPPLIER (SNO, LOCATION)
> SUPPLY (LNO, SNO, PNO, DESTINATION)

It consists of named files with named attributes. Secondary keys and relationships are conspicuously absent, characterizing the major differences from the network model. Secondary keys are not indicated, since in a relational structure all attributes are assumed to be secondary keys. This assumption requires index files and an access structure with respect to each attribute, greatly inflating the cost of relational systems. Relationships are not indicated, since they are implicit in the attribute values, and they are generated at run time by the system by comparing attribute values. For example, the SS relationship of Chapter 7 between the SUPPLIER and SUPPLY files can be generated by matching the SNO values in the two files. The advantage of this approach is that the user is not restricted to the predefined relationships but can generate any conceivable relationship by comparing attribute values. There are no restrictions as to what attributes can be used and what comparison operations can be applied since all attributes are secondary keys and hence can be used as search criteria. For example, it is possible to link each supplier with the supplies of other suppliers (SNO≠SNO), or it is possible to link each supplier with its local shipments (SNO = SNO, LOCATION = DESTINATION). It is even possible to create meaningless relationships by matching arbitrary attributes such as linking each supplier to the supplies of parts with PNO equal to the SNO of the supplier. Clearly, the additional power afforded to the users by such high level models can be misused or even abused. Users need effective data description to exercise the newly acquired power responsible, and they need to be monitored to prevent abuse.

The elimination of secondary keys and relationships leave stand-alone files as the only component of the logical structures. The files are viewed as simple named tables with named columns. The elimination of branching and looping results in languages that operate on complete files as opposed to individual records. A database system is considered relational if all data are viewed as named tables with named columns (and no additional structures), and all commands of the data language operate on tables (as opposed to individual records). Consequently, structural components such as relationships, secondary keys, index files, pointers, overflow areas, and language components such as loops, if statements, and assignment of values to variables all violate relational principles.

Relational systems have a terminology based on set theory, and it is different from the network terminology. In particular, a file is called a *relation* (not a relationship); an attribute is called a *domain;* a record is a *tuple;* the number of attributes in a file is referred to as its *degree;* the number of records in a file is its *cardinality;* and finally a one-to-many relationship is called a *function.* The basis for this terminology will be clear in the next section. Some commercially available relational systems are **SYSTEM R** of IBM, and **INGRES** of Relational Technology, Inc.

## Relational Algebra

A quick review of set algebra is appropriate at this point since set theory provides the basis for the relational model and the relational terminology; and relational algebra, the first major language of relational systems, is based on set algebra. A *set* is a named collection of objects. Three sets named BOY, GIRL, and TOY are given in Example 8.1. The cartesian product of two sets $A \times B$ is a set of all pairs where the first element of the pair is from the first set $A$ and the second element is from the second set $B$. A subset of the cartesian product is called a relation. Two relations named LOVE and HATE defined on BOY $\times$ GIRL, and a relation named OWN defined on GIRL $\times$ TOY are given in Example 8.1.

A set is also called a domain, and an element of the cartesian product is called a tuple. It is important to note that a cartesian product is a set of tuples, and so is a relation. A relation $R(A,B)$ is called a *function* from $A$ to $B$ if for every element in $A$, R has exactly one corresponding element in $B$. For example, LOVE is a function from GIRL to BOY, but not from BOY to GIRL. The number of domains defining a relation

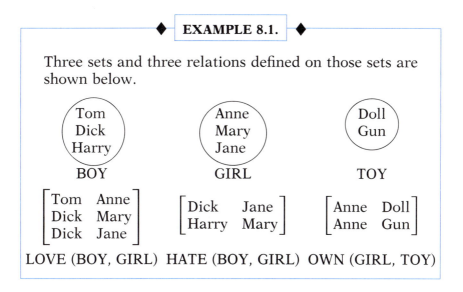

♦ **EXAMPLE 8.1.** ♦

Three sets and three relations defined on those sets are shown below.

|        |        |
|--------|--------|
| Tom    | Anne   | Doll |
| Dick   | Mary   | Gun  |
| Harry  | Jane   |      |
| BOY    | GIRL   | TOY  |

$$\begin{bmatrix} \text{Tom} & \text{Anne} \\ \text{Dick} & \text{Mary} \\ \text{Dick} & \text{Jane} \end{bmatrix} \quad \begin{bmatrix} \text{Dick} & \text{Jane} \\ \text{Harry} & \text{Mary} \end{bmatrix} \quad \begin{bmatrix} \text{Anne} & \text{Doll} \\ \text{Anne} & \text{Gun} \end{bmatrix}$$

LOVE (BOY, GIRL)  HATE (BOY, GIRL)  OWN (GIRL, TOY)

is called its degree. LOVE is a relation of degree 2. The number of elements in a set is called its cardinality. LOVE is of cardinality 3. Since relations are sets, the set operations apply to them. Union of two sets is a set containing all elements of either set; the intersection of two sets is a set containing the elements common to both sets, the subtraction of one set from another returns a set containing all elements of the second set except the ones also contained in the first.

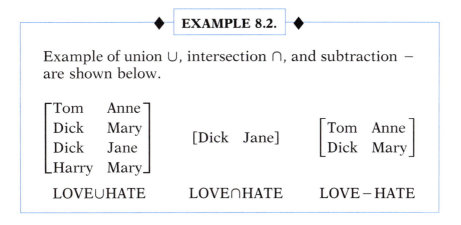

♦ **EXAMPLE 8.2.** ♦

Example of union ∪, intersection ∩, and subtraction − are shown below.

$$\begin{bmatrix} \text{Tom} & \text{Anne} \\ \text{Dick} & \text{Mary} \\ \text{Dick} & \text{Jane} \\ \text{Harry} & \text{Mary} \end{bmatrix} \quad [\text{Dick} \quad \text{Jane}] \quad \begin{bmatrix} \text{Tom} & \text{Anne} \\ \text{Dick} & \text{Mary} \end{bmatrix}$$

LOVE∪HATE        LOVE∩HATE        LOVE − HATE

In addition to the set operations, relational algebra contains three relational operations. *Projection* is used to identify and retrieve some columns of a relation, *restriction* is used to identify and retrieve some rows of a relation, and *join* is used to combine two relations to build a third relation by attaching certain rows from the first relation to certain rows of the second relation to form the rows of the new relation. Attaching of two rows to create a longer row is called *concatenation*.

◆ **EXAMPLE 8.3.** ◆

Given the relations LOVE and OWN of Example 8.1, the projection LOVE [BOY] returns the BOY column of LOVE; the restriction LOVE [BOY = DICK] returns the rows where the BOY value is Dick; and the join of LOVE and OWN LOVE[GIRL = GIRL]OWN creates a new relation where each row is a concatenation of a row from LOVE and a row from OWN where GIRL values are the same. This operation obviously relates some rows in LOVE relation to some rows in the OWN relation. In this respect it performs the same role as the relationships of network systems. The related rows are established by the condition in square brackets. The results of these operations are shown below.

$$\begin{bmatrix} \text{Tom} \\ \text{Dick} \end{bmatrix} \quad \begin{bmatrix} \text{Dick} & \text{Mary} \\ \text{Dick} & \text{Jane} \end{bmatrix} \quad \begin{bmatrix} \text{Tom} & \text{Anne} & \text{Anne} & \text{Doll} \\ \text{Tom} & \text{Anne} & \text{Anne} & \text{Gun} \end{bmatrix}$$

LOVE [BOY]   LOVE [BOY = DICK]   LOVE [GIRL = GIRL] OWN

More formally, relational algebra consists of seven operations, the first three of which are called *relational operations* and the remaining four are *set operations*. Given a relation R with domains $A_1$, $A_2$, . . . , $A_n$, and a relation B with domains $B_1$, $B_2$, . . . , $B_n$:

1. Projection $R[A_i, A_j, . . . , A_k]$ returns a relation that contains only the domains $A_i$, $A_j$, . . . , $A_k$ of the original relation.

2. Restriction $R[A_i \theta c]$ (or $R[A_i \theta A_j]$) returns a relation that contains only the tuples that satisfy the condition $A_i \theta c$ (or $A_i \theta A_j$) where $\theta$ is one of $=, \neq, <, \leq, >, \geq$ and c is a constant.

3. Join $R[A_i \theta B_j]S$ returns a relation whose tuples are formed by concatenating a tuple from R with a tuple from S whenever they meet the condition $A_i \theta B_j$.

4. Union $R \cup S$ returns a relation that contains both the tuples of R and the tuples of S.

5. Intersection $R \cap S$ returns a relation that contains the tuples which are common to both R and S.

6. Difference $R - S$ returns a relation that contains the tuples that are in R but not in S.

7. Cartesian product $R \times S$ returns a relation whose tuples are formed by concatenating a tuple from R with a tuple from S for all tuples. A join is always a subset of the corresponding cartesian product since the cartesian product contains all possible combinations but the join contains only those combinations that satisfy its condition.

Relational algebra expressions consist of consecutive applications of these operations executed from left to right, except that the relational operations have precedence over the set operations (i.e., relational operations are executed before set operations).

**EXAMPLE 8.4.**

The following relational algebra expressions demonstrate all operations of the language, given the two relations SUPPLIER (SNO, LOC) and SUPPLY (SNO, PNO) containing the supplier number and location of each supplier, and supplier number and part number of each supply in a manufacturing environment:

1. Suppliers of part 1121:

    SUPPLY[PNO = 1121][SNO]

2. Suppliers of a part other than 1121:

    SUPPLY[PNO ≠ 1121][SNO]

3. Suppliers of part 1121 or part 1790:

    SUPPLY[PNO = 1121][SNO] ∪
        SUPPLY[PNO = 1790][SNO]

4. Suppliers of part 1121 and part 1790:

    SUPPLY[PNO = 1121][SNO] ∩
        SUPPLY[PNO = 1790][SNO]

5. Suppliers who do not supply part 1121:

    SUPPLIER[SNO] − SUPPLY[PNO = 1121][SNO]

6. Suppliers who supply part 1121 but not part 1790:

SUPPLY[PNO = 1121][SNO] − SUPPLY[PNO = 1790][SNO]

7. The locations that supply part 1121:

SUPPLIER[SNO = SNO']SUPPLY'[PNO' = 1121][LOC]

where SUPPLY'(SNO', PNO') is assumed to be a copy of SUPPLY (SNO, PNO). Multiple copies of files are used to distinguish the columns with identical names created by join operation.

8.  Suppliers who supply all parts:

    SUPPLY[SNO] − (SUPPLY[SNO] ×
                SUPPLY[PNO] − SUPPLY)[SNO]

    where the cartesian product returns all possible
    SNO, PNO pairs. SUPPLY can be viewed as the
    set of all valid SNO, PNO pairs where SNO sup-
    plies PNO. Subtraction returns the invalid pairs
    where SNO does not supply PNO. Projection re-
    turns the suppliers participating in invalid pairs,
    i.e., the suppliers who failed to supply at least
    one part. All other suppliers are the suppliers
    who supplied all parts.

Relational algebra is a powerful and concise language. It is
very popular with analysts and academics. Unfortunately, end
users find its algebraic notation unfamiliar and imposing. Relational algebra also becomes unwieldy for more complex
questions. It is claimed that its complexity does not increase
proportionally, but faster, as the complexity perceived by humans increases. To alleviate these concerns, a second standard
language, relational calculus, is introduced.

## Relational Calculus

Relational calculus is based on the predicate calculus of first-
order logic. It is used to describe the subset of the database to
be returned as an answer to a query, rather than giving instructions to the system how to compute that answer. This type of
language is called a *declarative* or *nonprocedural* language,
since it declares the conditions the response should satisfy,
rather than expressing the procedures to be used to retrieve it.

In short, they state what is to be retrieved but not how it is to be retrieved. They are characterized by a lack of sequencing of operations that was so typical of relational algebra. Relational calculus does not impose a sequence of operations, since its operators are descriptive, merely providing the constraints the response should satisfy.

Predicate calculus provides three major logical operations AND $\wedge$, OR $\vee$, and IMPLICATION $\rightarrow$, and two quantifiers THERE EXISTS $\exists$, and FOR EVERY $\forall$. A quick review of these operations is useful before studying relational calculus. A *predicate* is a relationship that may be true or false for each value associated with its arguments.

---

◆ **EXAMPLE 8.5.** ◆

Some typical predicates are CARRY$(x,y)$ meaning "$x$ carries $y$," DRY$(x)$ meaning $x$ is dry, R meaning "it is raining," and INDOORS$(x)$ meaning $x$ is indoors. Predicates can have 0, 1, or more arguments as in this example. Predicates with zero arguments are called *propositions*.

---

Simple expressions are predicates combined with $\wedge$, $\vee$, or $\rightarrow$. Given two predicates P and Q, P$\wedge$Q means both P and Q must be true, P$\vee$Q means either P or Q or both must be true, P$\rightarrow$Q means if P is true then Q must be true. The following table shows the possibilities involved.

| $P$ | $Q$ | $P \wedge Q$ | $P \vee Q$ | $P \rightarrow Q$ |
|-----|-----|------|------|------|
| T | T | T | T | T |
| T | F | F | T | F |
| F | T | F | T | T |
| F | F | F | F | T |

---

♦ **EXAMPLE 8.6.** ♦

Some typical simple expressions are:

R∧DRY(john)  meaning "it is raining and john is dry";
CARRY(john,umbrella)∨INDOORS(john)  meaning "either john is carrying an umbrella or john is indoors or both";
R→CARRY(john,umbrella)  meaning "if it is raining then john carries an umbrella";
(R∧DRY(john))→(CARRY(john,umbrella)∨INDOORS (john))  meaning "if it is raining and john is dry, then either john is carrying an umbrella or he is indoors or both."

---

*Quantified expressions* are simple expressions combined with ∃ or ∀. Given a simple expression, P($x$), ∃$x$P($x$) means there is at least one value for $x$ for which P($x$) is true; ∀$x$P($x$) means for every value of $x$ P($x$) is true.

---

♦ **EXAMPLE 8.7.** ♦

Some typical quantified expressions are given below, assuming the variable $x$ refers to people and the variable $y$ refers to things:

∃$y$ CARRY(john,$y$) meaning "john is carrying something";
∃$x$ CARRY($x$,umbrella) meaning "somebody is carrying an umbrella";
∀$x$ INDOORS($x$) meaning "everybody is indoors";
∀$x$ INDOORS($x$)∨CARRY($x$,umbrella) meaning "everybody is either indoors or carrying an umbrella";
∀$x$(INDOORS($x$)∨CARRY($x$,umbrella))→DRY($x$) meaning "everybody who is inside or carries an umbrella is dry";
∀$x$∃$y$ CARRY($x$,$y$) meaning "everybody carries something";

**EXAMPLE 8.7.** (*Continued*)

$\exists y \forall x$ CARRY($x,y$) meaning "there is something that everybody carries";

$\exists y \forall x$ (INDOORS($x$)$\lor$CARRY($x,y$))$\rightarrow$DRY($x$) meaning there is something that can keep you dry if you carry it; being indoors also keeps you dry. Either condition or both is sufficient to keep you dry."

A relational calculus expression is merely a predicate calculus expression where each predicate is of the type R.$A\theta$c or R.$A\theta$S.$B$ where R and S are relations; $A$ and $B$ are their attributes, respectively; c is a constant; and $\theta$ is a comparison operator such as =, $\neq$, <, $\leq$, >, $\geq$. Relation names are used as variables spanning the rows of each relation. A relational calculus query is of the type R.$A$:E where E is a relational calculus expression, and the query is interpreted to return the $A$ value for each row of R, if E returns "true" for that row of R.

◆ **EXAMPLE 8.8.** ◆

The following relational calculus queries demonstrate all operators of the language, given two relations SUPPLIER(SNO,LOC) and SUPPLY(SNO,PNO) containing the supplier number and location of each supplier, and the supplier number and part number of each supply in a manufacturing environment.

1. Suppliers of part 1121:

$$\text{SUPPLY.SNO:SUPPLY.PNO} = 1121$$

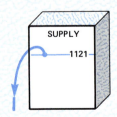

2. Suppliers of a part other than 1121:

$$\text{SUPPLY.SNO:SUPPLY.PNO} \neq 1121$$

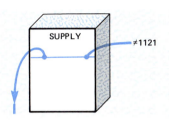

3. Suppliers of part 1121 or part 1790:

$$\text{SUPPLY.SNO:SUPPLY.PNO} = 1121 \lor$$
$$\text{SUPPLY.PNO} = 1790$$

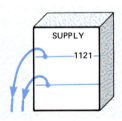

4. The locations that supply part 1121:

$$\text{SUPPLIER.LOC:]SUPPLY}$$
$$\text{SUPPLY.SNO} = \text{SUPPLIER.SNO}$$

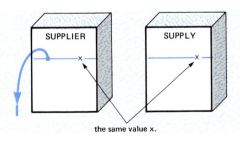

the same value x.

**EXAMPLE 8.8.** (*Continued*)

5. The suppliers of part 1121 and part 1790:

   SUPPLY.SNO:∃SUPPLY'
   SUPPLY.SNO = SUPPLY'.SNO∧
   SUPPLY.PNO = 1121∧SUPPLY'.PNO = 1790

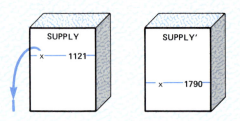

   where SUPPLY and SUPPLY' represent two distinct variables spanning the rows of the relation SUPPLY.

6. The supplier who supplies all the supplies:

   SUPPLIER.SNO:∀
           SUPPLY SUPPLIER.SNO = SUPPLY.SNO

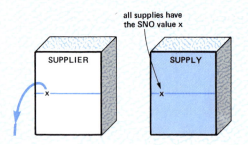

7. The suppliers who do not supply part 1121:

   SUPPLIER.SNO:∀SUPPLY
   SUPPLIER.SNO = SUPPLY.SNO→SUPPLY.PNO≠1121

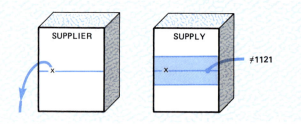

8. The suppliers who supply part 1121, but not part 1790:

SUPPLY.SNO:∀SUPPLY' SUPPLY.PNO = 1121∧
(SUPPLY.SNO = SUPPLY'.SNO→

SUPPLY'.PNO≠1790)

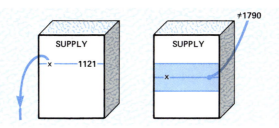

9. The suppliers who supply all parts:

SUPPLIER.SNO:∀SUPPLY∃SUPPLY'
SUPPLY.PNO = SUPPLY'.PNO∧

SUPPLY'.SNO = SUPPLIER.SNO

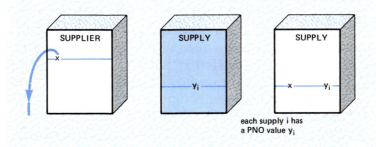

each supply i has
a PNO value y$_i$

where the SUPPLY file is used to provide the list of all parts, and SUPPLY' is used to check if each one of those parts is supplied by a supplier.

The similarity of relational calculus expressions to English expressions is striking. With some experience most relational calculus expressions can be read as if they were English sentences. Actually, there have been attempts to translate English queries into relational calculus, thus allowing users to enter their queries in English with no restrictions. These attempts have largely failed due to ambiguities in natural languages.

Database querying requires precision and like many other activities that require precision, free-style natural language is not appropriate for it. Many fields ranging from law to music, medicine to military, and architecture to mathematics have developed special notations for activities involving precision. Database querying is no exception. It is important to remember that computers are there to take orders from humans, not to chat with them.

## *RBASE*

RBASE was originally designed for the National Aeronautics and Space Administration (NASA) under the name Relational Information Management (RIM). Its microcomputer version is developed and marketed by MICRO RIM, Inc. of Bellevue, Washington. It is an excellent example of relational algebra. It is almost identical to the standard form except for replacing operators with English keywords and naming intermediate results. Projection and restriction are combined into a single PROJECT command with a subcommand USING corresponding to projection, and the subcommand WHERE corresponding to restriction. Join is accomplished by a JOIN operator, and similarly set operations UNION, INTERSECT, and SUBTRACT are provided. The cartesian product is not provided, and it has to be derived using two complementary joins and a union. SELECT is used to print the results and REMOVE to clean up all the intermediate relations. RENAME is used to change the names of fields to create multiple copies. Translation is straightforward and the following examples demonstrate RBASE given the same manufacturing database.

◆ **EXAMPLE 8.9.** ◆

Suppliers of part 1121:

```
PROJECT A FROM SUPPLY USING SNO
                       WHERE PNO EQ 1121
SELECT ALL FROM A
REMOVE A
```

◆ **EXAMPLE 8.10.** ◆

Suppliers of a part other than 1121:

```
PROJECT A FROM SUPPLY USING SNO
                       WHERE PNO NE 1121
SELECT ALL FROM A
REMOVE A
```

◆ **EXAMPLE 8.11.** ◆

Suppliers of part 1121 or part 1790:

```
PROJECT A FROM SUPPLY USING SNO
                       WHERE PNO EQ 1121
PROJECT B FROM SUPPLY USING SNO
                       WHERE PNO EQ 1790
UNION A WITH B FORMING C
SELECT ALL FROM C
REMOVE C
```

◆ **EXAMPLE 8.12.** ◆

Suppliers of part 1121 and part 1790:

```
INTERSECT A WITH B FORMING C
SELECT ALL FROM C
REMOVE C
```

◆ **EXAMPLE 8.13.** ◆

Suppliers who do not supply part 1121:

```
PROJECT D FROM SUPPLIER USING SNO
SUBTRACT A FROM D FORMING C
SELECT ALL FROM C
REMOVE C
REMOVE D
```

◆ **EXAMPLE 8.14.** ◆

Suppliers who supply part 1121 but not part 1790:

```
SUBTRACT B FROM A FORMING C
SELECT ALL FROM C
REMOVE A
REMOVE B
REMOVE C
```

◆ **EXAMPLE 8.15.** ◆

The locations that supply part 1121:

```
RENAME SNO TO SNO1 IN SUPPLY
JOIN SUPPLIER USING SNO WITH SUPPLY USING
              SNO1 FORMING A WHERE EQ
PROJECT B FROM A USING LOC WHERE
                        PNO EQ 1121
SELECT ALL FROM B
REMOVE A
REMOVE B
RENAME SNO1 TO SNO IN SUPPLY
```

◆ **EXAMPLE 8.16.** ◆

Suppliers who supply all parts:

```
PROJECT A FROM SUPPLY USING SNO
PROJECT B FROM SUPPLY USING PNO
JOIN A USING SNO WITH B USING PNO
                    FORMING C WHERE LE
JOIN A USING SNO WITH B USING PNO
                    FORMING D WHERE GT
UNION C WITH D FORMING E
SUBTRACT SUPPLY FROM E FORMING F
PROJECT G FROM F USING SNO
SUBTRACT G FROM A FORMING H
SELECT ALL FROM H
REMOVE H
REMOVE G
REMOVE F
REMOVE E
REMOVE D
REMOVE C
REMOVE B
REMOVE A
```

## *Structured Query Language*

Structured Query Language (SQL) was originally developed by IBM under the name SEQUEL (Structured English Query Language). It has achieved wide acceptance and it is available from a variety of vendors for a variety of mainframes and microcomputers. SQL front ends for most major database systems are in the market, and ORACLE of San Jose, California provides a stand-alone SQL product for most microcomputers. SQL provides a reasonable example of relational calculus although translation at times is not straightforward, largely because SQL does not provide for every "$\forall$" quantifier, but a not exists "$\sim\exists$" instead, and the expressions often need to be negated for translation. Moreover, the implication $\rightarrow$ operator is not available and $\rightarrow$ has to be translated to $\wedge$ and $\vee$. The following rules of translation are employed to bring relational calculus expressions into an acceptable form by SQL:

$$
\begin{array}{cc}
\forall & \sim\exists\sim \\
A \rightarrow B & \sim A \vee B \\
\sim(A \vee B) & \sim A \wedge \sim B \\
\sim(A \wedge B) & \sim A \vee \sim B
\end{array}
$$

For example, $\forall x \exists y \forall z\ (A \rightarrow B)$ goes through the following transformation:

$$
\begin{array}{l}
\forall x \exists y \forall z\ (A \rightarrow B) \\
\sim\exists x \sim\exists y \sim\exists z \sim (A \rightarrow B) \\
\sim\exists x \sim\exists y \sim\exists z \sim (\sim A \vee B) \\
\sim\exists x \exists y \sim\exists z \sim (A \wedge \sim B)
\end{array}
$$

Another example is $\forall x \forall y\ A \wedge B \rightarrow C$:

$$
\begin{array}{l}
\forall x \forall y\ (A \wedge B \rightarrow C) \\
\sim\exists x \sim\sim\exists y \sim (A \wedge B \rightarrow C) \\
\sim\exists x \exists y \sim (\sim A \vee \sim B \vee C) \\
\sim\exists x \exists y\ (A \wedge B \wedge \sim C)
\end{array}
$$

Once in the correct form the expressions can be written in SQL simply by replacing the operators with the corresponding English keywords. The correspondence is as follows:

| | |
|---|---|
| SUPPLY.SNO: | SELECT SUPPLY.SNO<br>FROM SUPPLY<br>WHERE |
| SUPPLY.SNO: ꓕSUPPLIER | SELECT SUPPLY.SNO<br>FROM SUPPLY, SUPPLIER<br>WHERE |
| ~ꓕSUPPLY _____ | NOT EXISTS<br>(SELECT * FROM SUPPLY<br>WHERE _____) |

The following examples, each corresponding to a question in Example 8.8, demonstrate SQL and the translation from relational calculus. Note that all SQL expressions end with a semicolon (;):

◆ **EXAMPLE 8.17.** ◆

Suppliers of part 1121.
SUPPLY.SNO: SUPPLY.PNO = 1121

```
SELECT SUPPLY.SNO
FROM SUPPLY
WHERE SUPPLY.PNO=1121;
```

◆ **EXAMPLE 8.18.** ◆

Suppliers of a part other than 1121:
SUPPLY.SNO: SUPPLY.PNO≠1121

```
SELECT SUPPLY.SNO
FROM SUPPLY
WHERE SUPPLY.PNO≠1121;
```

---

◆ **EXAMPLE 8.19.** ◆

Suppliers of part 1121 or part 1790:
SUPPLY.SNO: SUPPLY.PNO = 1121∨
SUPPLY.PNO = 1790

```
SELECT SUPPLY.SNO
FROM SUPPLY
WHERE SUPPLY.PNO=1121
OR SUPPLY.PNO=1790;
```

---

◆ **EXAMPLE 8.20.** ◆

The locations that supply part 1121:
SUPPLIER.LOC: ∃SUPPLY
SUPPLY.SNO = SUPPLIER.SNO∧SUPPLY.PNO = 1121

```
SELECT SUPPLIER.LOC
FROM SUPPLIER, SUPPLY
WHERE SUPPLIER.SNO=SUPPLY.SNO
AND SUPPLY.PNO=1121;
```

---

◆ **EXAMPLE 8.21.** ◆

The suppliers of part 1121 and part 1790:
SUPPLY.SNO: ∃SUPPLY′SUPPLY.SNO =
SUPPLY′.SNO∧SUPPLY.PNO = 1121∧
SUPPLY′.PNO = 1790

```
SELECT SUPPLY.SNO
FROM SUPPLY, SUPPLY1
WHERE SUPPLY.SNO=SUPPLY1.SNO
AND SUPPLY. PNO=1121
AND SUPPLY1.PNO=1790;
```

Note that SUPPLY1 must be created as a duplicate of
SUPPLY.

---

---

◆ **EXAMPLE 8.22.** ◆

---

The supplier who supplied all the supplies:
SUPPLIER.SNO: ~∃ SUPPLY
                       SUPPLIER.SNO≠SUPPLY.SNO

```
SELECT SUPPLIER.SNO
FROM SUPPLIER
WHERE NOT EXISTS
 (SELECT * FROM SUPPLY
 WHERE SUPPLIER.SNO <> SUPPLY.SNO);
```

---

◆ **EXAMPLE 8.23.** ◆

---

The suppliers who do not supply part 1121:
SUPPLIER.SNO: ~∃ SUPPLY
SUPPLIER.SNO = SUPPLY.SNO∧SUPPLY.PNO = 1121

```
SELECT SUPPLIER.SNO
FROM SUPPLIER
WHERE NOT EXISTS
 (SELECT * FROM SUPPLY
 WHERE SUPPLIER.SNO=SUPPLY.SNO
 AND SUPPLY.PNO=1121);
```

---

◆ **EXAMPLE 8.24.** ◆

---

The suppliers who supply part 1121, but not part 1790:
SUPPLY.SNO: ~∃SUPPLY'SUPPLY.PNO≠1121∨
(SUPPLY.SNO = SUPPLY'.SNO∧SUPPLY'.PNO = 1790)

```
SELECT SUPPLY.SNO
FROM SUPPLY
WHERE NOT EXISTS
 (SELECT * FROM SUPPLY1
 WHERE SUPPLY.PNO <> 1121
 OR (SUPPLY.SNO=SUPPLY1.SNO
 AND SUPPLY1.PNO=1790));
```

---

◆ **EXAMPLE 8.25.** ◆

Suppliers who supply all parts:
SUPPLIER.SNO:~]SUPPLY~]SUPPLY'SUPPLY.PNO =
    SUPPLY'.PNO∧SUPPLY'.SNO = SUPPLIER.SNO

```
SELECT SUPPLIER.SNO
FROM SUPPLIER
WHERE NOT EXISTS
  (SELECT * FROM SUPPLY
  WHERE NOT EXISTS
    (SELECT * FROM SUPPLY1
    WHERE SUPPLY.PNO=SUPPLY1.PNO
    AND SUPPLY1.SNO=SUPPLIER.SNO));
```

## QUESTIONS

1. Given the following database for a manufacturing environment:

> SUPPLIER (SNO,NAME,LOC)
> PART (PNO,TYPE,PRICE,WEIGHT)
> PROJECT (JNO,LOC,TEC)
> SUPPLY (LNO,SNO,PNO,JNO,QUANTITY,DATE)

containing the supplier number, name and location of each supplier; part number, part type, part price and weight for each part; project number, project location and the total estimated cost for each project receiving parts; and supply number, supplier number, part number, project number, quantity, and date for each supply. Write relational algebra expressions for the following queries:
a. Suppliers in Chicago
b. Parts supplied by supplier 210
c. Parts supplied by a supplier other than 210

d. Parts supplied by supplier 210 or 206
e. Parts supplied by supplier 210 and 206
f. Parts supplied from Chicago
g. Parts supplied from Chicago to Chicago
h. Part types supplied
i. Parts not supplied to project 14
j. Part types not supplied
k. Parts of type C supplied by supplier 212 to project 14
l. Parts supplied to all projects

2. Write relational calculus expressions for the same queries.

3. Locate a commercial relational system that supports relational algebra such as DBASE or Micro Rim's RBASE. Create the database of Question 1 in your system, and load the following data:

```
SUPPLIER(SNO,NAME,LOC)
        206 ACE MILWAUKEE
        210 NATIONAL CHICAGO
        212 UNIVERSAL NEWYORK
        214 ARTS MILWAUKEE
PART(PNO,TYPE,PRICE,WEIGHT)
        1017 A    11.26    62
        1121 B     2.00    11
        1790 C     6.50    70
        1212 A    11.26    25
PROJECT(JNO,LOC,TEC)
        10 MILWAUKEE 10000
        12 CHICAGO    45000
        14 CHICAGO    25000
        16 NEWYORK    12500
SUPPLY(LNO,SNO,PNO,JNO,QUANTITY,DATE)
        1   206  1121   14   500    70188
        7   210  1790   10   600   100188
        5   210  1121   12   400    61588
        6   212  1790   14   700    70188
        8   212  1121   10   200    70188
        9   212  1121   16   400    70188
```

4. Identify the differences between your system and standard relational algebra. Enter the queries of Question 1 into your system. Debug and execute the queries.

5. Locate a commercial relational system that supports Relational Calculus or a similar language such as SQL or INGRES's QUEL. Create the database of Question 1 in your system and load the data provided in Question 3.

6. Identify the differences between your system and standard relational calculus. Enter the queries of Question 1 into your system. Debug and execute your queries.

7. Repeat questions 1 and 2 for the following queries:
   a. Suppliers of exactly one part
   b. Suppliers of at least two parts
   c. Suppliers of exactly two parts
   d. Suppliers of at most two parts

8. Predicate calculus is often used to eliminate ambiguities inherent in natural languages. The following is a list of proposals considered by the common council of a small town as a possible wording of the ordinance to eliminate free-roaming dogs from the city park. Try to write each in predicate calculus and show why it is wrong.
   a. "No dogs must be brought to this park except on a leash," which does not prevent a dog owner from releasing his dog once safely inside the park.
   b. "Dogs are not allowed in this park without leashes," which is an ordinance directed at dogs but not the owners, and consequently may allow only the prosecution of violating dogs. Moreover, it does not require the existence of a human holding the leash.
   c. "Owners of dogs are not allowed in this park unless they keep their dogs on leashes," which prevents a dog owner from leaving his dog in his backyard at home, and going for a walk in the park.
   d. "Nobody without his dog on a leash is allowed in this park," which prevents a citizen who does not own a dog from walking in the park without acquiring one.

e. "Dogs must be on leash in this park," which sounds like
a general injunction to the residents of the city to bring
their dogs into the park.

f. "All dogs in this park must be kept on leash."

## BIBLIOGRAPHY

Date, C. J. *An Introduction to Database Systems.* Reading, MA:
Addison-Wesley Publishing Co. Inc., 1986.

Elmasri, R., Navathe, S. B. *Fundamentals of Database Systems.*
Menlo Park, CA: Benjamin Cummings, 1989.

Ullman, J. D. *Principles of Database Systems.* Rockville, MD:
Computer Science Press Inc., 1982.

*Chapter 9*

♦

# Functional Model

The functional model of data is an object oriented data model. It goes one step further away from the physical structure by eliminating the concept of file as a physical collection of attributes where each record corresponds to a real-world entity. In an object oriented data model the real-world entities are represented directly by internal objects, and each attribute is a function from a set of objects to printable character strings that describe those objects. A *functional structure* is a collection of functions defined on object sets where each object set corresponds to an entity type in real life. A functional structure is given below for a typical manufacturing environment. All functions defined on the same object set are listed together separated by commas.

> SNO,LOCATION(SUPPLIER)
> LNO,DESTINATION,SUPPLIER,PART(SUPPLY)

The functional model maintains all the advantages of the relational system. In addition, it eliminates the need for keys to uniquely identify entities, and eliminates the implicit correspondence between relations and flat physical files by allowing multiple values of an attribute to be modeled directly as multivalued functions. Functions are smaller units of data than relations, and using smaller units has advantages in end user–oriented languages and in interfacing with procedures. The major contribution of the functional model to end user orientation is in visual languages, to be discussed in the next section.

## *Visual Data Model*

Visual Data Model (VDM) expresses all structures and queries using geometric shapes such as rectangles, arcs, and circles. It is based on the functional model of data, and each object set is denoted by a rectangle, and each function by an arc.

---

◆ | **EXAMPLE 9.1.** | ◆

The visual structure corresponding to a simple manu-facturing environment is given below. There are two entity types, and five functions defined on them, one linking the two entity types.

SNO,LOC(SUPPLIER)
LNO,PNO,SUPPLIER(SUPPLY)

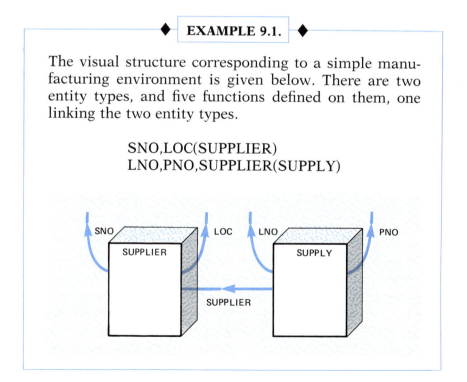

Visual Data Language (VDL) is used in conjunction with the Visual Data Model. Its expressions are visual, consisting of arcs, rectangles, and circles. The major component of VDL is a labeled arc connecting two data points, where the points correspond to data items and the arc corresponds to a function relating the two data items.

◆ **EXAMPLE 9.2.** ◆

"s is a supplier of shipment p" is expressed as follows:

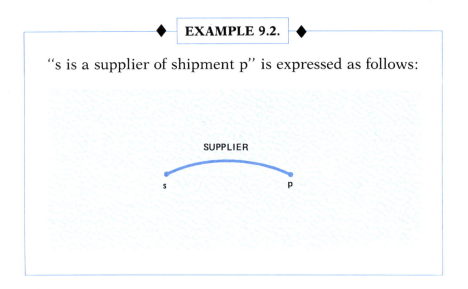

Labeled rectangles are used to represent entity sets, and arcs can link rectangles as well as points. Arcs linking rectangles correspond to the quantifiers of the first-order logic.

◆ **EXAMPLE 9.3.** ◆

The following four diagrams represent the statements "s supplies something," "s supplies everything," "s supplies nothing," and "s supplies a subset of all shipments":

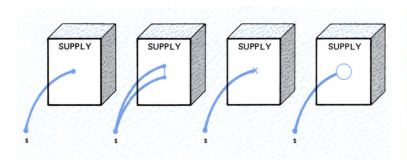

The last construct is the same as the first except that the circle represents all supplies by s, and it can be used for subsetting operations by combining it with other constructs. Connected double points (•—•) represent all objects in a data set. The two points can be viewed as the two representative objects of all objects in the data set, and their relationships are considered representative of all the objects. A VDL query is a combination of these four constructs with dangling arrows indicating the data items to be returned.

◆ **EXAMPLE 9.4.** ◆

The following queries demonstrate the use of VDL, given the data model of Example 9.1:

1.   Suppliers of part 1121:

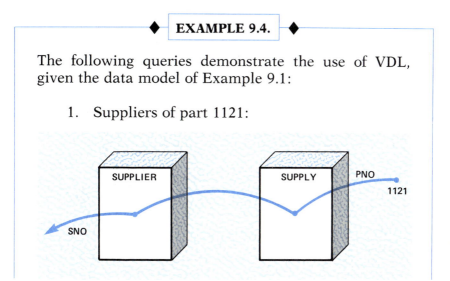

**EXAMPLE 9.4** (*Continued*)

2.  Suppliers of a part other than 1121:

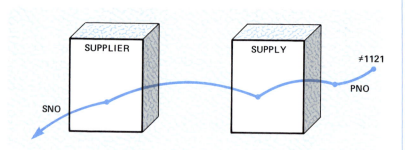

3.  Suppliers of part 1121 or part 1790:

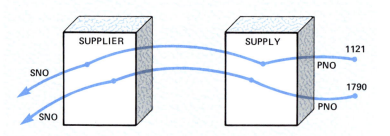

4.  The locations that supply part 1121:

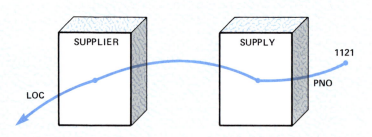

5.  The suppliers of part 1121 and part 1790:

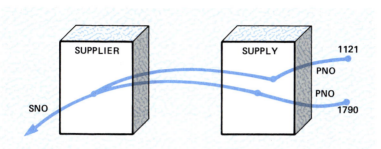

6.  The supplier who supplied all supplies:

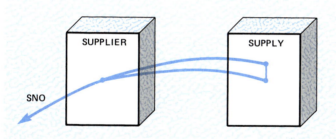

7.  The suppliers who do not supply part 1121:

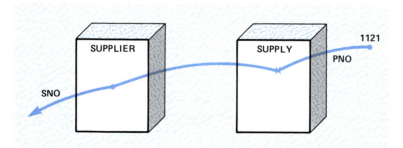

**EXAMPLE 9.4** (*Continued*)

8.  The suppliers who supply part 1121 but not 1790:

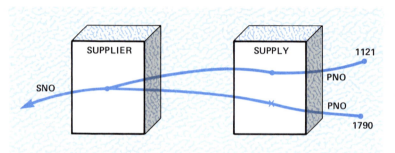

9.  The suppliers who supply all shipments of part 1121:

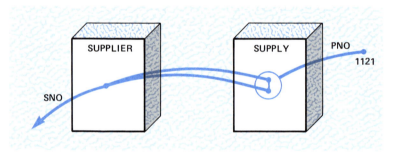

10.  The suppliers who supply all parts:

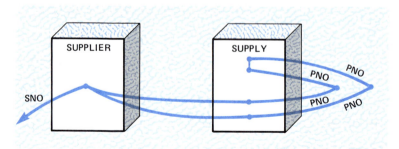

> where the supplier is expected to supply at least one shipment of a given part. This process is repeated for each part where the part list is given by the SUPPLY file.

For most queries, the visual data model and the VDL expressions are intuitive and they can be used with relatively little training. They are most appropriate for office workers with little or no technical training and little understanding of database concepts.

## QUESTIONS

1. Given the following functional data model for a manufacturing environment:

   SNO,NAME,LOC(SUPPLIER)
   PNO.TYPE,PRICE,WEIGHT(PART)
   JNO,LOC,TEC(PROJECT)
   LNO,SUPPLIER,PART,PROJECT,QUANTITY,DATE(SUPPLY)

   containing the supplier number, name, and location of each supplier; part number, type, price, and weight of each part; project number, location, and total estimated cost of each project; supply number, supplier, part supplied, project receiving the supply, quantity and date of each supply.
   Express this structure using the visual data model.

2. Draw VDL expressions for the following queries:
   a. Suppliers in Chicago
   b. Parts supplied by supplier 210
   c. Parts supplied by a supplier other than 210
   d. Parts supplied by supplier 210 or 206
   e. Parts supplied by supplier 210 and 206

   f. Parts supplied from Chicago

   g. Parts supplied from Chicago to Chicago

   h. Part types supplied

   i. Parts not supplied to project 14

   j. Part types not supplied

   k. Parts of type A supplied by supplier 212 to project 14

   l. Parts supplied to all projects

## BIBLIOGRAPHY

Chang, S. K. *Principles of Visual Programming Systems.* Englewood Cliffs, NJ: Prentice-Hall, 1990.

Cox, B. J. *Object Oriented Programming: An Evolutionary Approach.* Reading, MA: Addison-Wesley Publishing Co. Inc., 1986.

Elmasri, R., Navathe, S. B. *Fundamentals of Database Systems.* Menlo Park, CA: Benjamin-Cummings, 1989.

Orman, L. Functional development of database applications. *Transactions on Software Engineering,* 14(9):1280–1292, 1988.

# Chapter 10

◆

# Database Design

*Database design* is the process of translating the data needs of an organization to a logical data structure acceptable to a database management system. It is the first step of building an organizational database, and it usually is a long and tedious process for any nontrivial organization. The difficulty is implied by the fact that a database is a shared organizational resource, and has to satisfy the data needs of many constituencies within the organization. These needs are often diverse and sometimes conflicting. The general philosophy of database design is to capture all data needs of the organization, and to build a structure to respond to them all effectively.

The first phase of database design involves the use of a variety of informal tools to capture and clarify the data needs. The most commonly used tools in this phase are entity-relationship (E-R) diagrams and data dictionaries. The second phase of the design process involves converting the captured data needs to a logical structure. This phase requires a strategy for evaluating and comparing different logical structures to choose the best among all acceptable alternatives. The most commonly used tool for this formal analysis is normalization. These tools are introduced in this chapter with a running example of a university registration system.

## Entity-Relationship Diagrams

An E-R diagram is an informal tool to capture the data needs of an organization. It is relatively easy to draw and to read, and hence it facilitates communication among designers and users. It contains the answers to three basic questions in a graphical form. The three questions are

1. What are the things of interest? These are the real-life things about which the organization would like to collect information. They are called *entities*.

2. What information should be collected about each entity? These are called *attributes*.

3. What relationships exist among the entities?

E-R diagrams simply indicate the entities by rectangles, attributes by circles, and the relationships by diamonds as in Example 10.1.

Not all E-R diagrams are equally useful. Some are better than others. The criteria to judge E-R diagrams are completeness and nonredundancy. A good E-R diagram is expected to be complete and nonredundant. Completeness is obviously important to respond to all needs, and nonredundancy is important to insure that the same need is not captured in multiple places in different forms, thus causing conflicts and inconsistencies. Nonredundancy is the major objective of normalization and will be studied in detail in the Normalization section.

The E-R diagram of Example 10.1 demonstrates a number of important points.

1. Grade is an attribute of the enrollment relationship between STUDENT and COURSE. It could have been captured as an attribute of STUDENT, in which case a set of grades would be associated with each student, but the information about which grade corresponds to which course would have been lost.

**◆ EXAMPLE 10.1. ◆**

The E-R diagram for a university registration system is shown below where the relevant entities are students, courses, and professors:

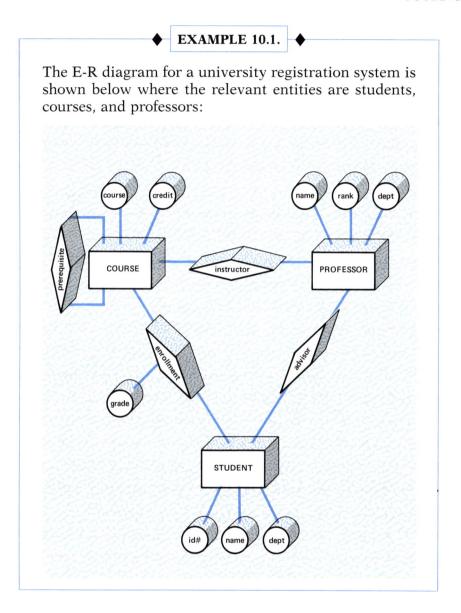

2. The grade point average (GPA) of each student would be redundant if included, since it can be derived from the grades of the student. Derived data do not belong in a logical structure, since they are always redundant

and computable from the observed data. Derived data are captured in derivation procedures, to be studied in Chapter 12.

3.  It is possible to have a reflexive relationship, i.e., a relationship connecting an entity set to itself. "Prerequisite" is such a relationship of the entity set COURSE to itself. It is not clear if "prerequisite" links each course to its immediate prerequisites or to its transitive closure, i.e., all courses that have to be taken prior to it.

4.  The semester of enrollment is missing. It should be added as an attribute of enrollment, if it is necessary to compute GPAs for each semester or to produce end-of-term grade reports.

5.  The department of a student may be redundant if it is the same as the department of her advisor.

6.  A course may have multiple instructors. It is not clear which professor is the instructor of a student in a given course. If this is a relevant piece of information, it can be captured by converting "instructor" to a relationship among all three entity sets. A relationship can link more than two entity sets.

## Data Dictionary

E-R Diagrams for real-life organizations can become very large and complex. For these diagrams to be effective as communication tools, it is important to use names that are commonly understood and correctly interpreted. A name such as "prerequisite," for example, may be interpreted in a variety of ways. To prevent ambiguities all names used in an E-R diagram are defined in detail in a dictionary. This data dictionary is similar to ordinary dictionaries. It may contain examples, synonyms, homonyms, and cross-references in addition to definitions.

Data dictionaries are also collections of data and may be included in the organizational database.

Some dictionaries go another step and attach keywords to each attribute describing the semantics of attributes. These keywords go a long way toward clarifying the intent of the designer by describing the behavior of data. Many of these keywords were suggested by semantic data models. The most commonly used keywords are

- *Mandatory:* It requires an attribute to take a value for each entity. No entity is allowed to have the null value for that attribute. A typical example is the id# for students.
- *Single-valued:* It requires an attribute to have at most one value for each attribute. Names of professors would be an example of a single-valued attribute.
- *Nonchangeable:* These attributes have fixed values. Once a value is assigned to a nonchangeable attribute, it cannot be modified. A typical example is the professors' departments in a university where interdepartmental transfers are not allowed.
- *Nonoverlapping:* These attributes have exclusive values for each attribute. In other words, if an attribute is non-overlapping, no two entities have a common value for that attribute. A typical example is course# where although a course may have multiple course# listings, a course# may belong only to one course.

## *Normalization*

*Normalization* is the formal phase of the design process. It starts where the informal process leaves off, by converting the E-R diagrams to a relational database, and then continues in five steps, identifying and eliminating a type of redundancy at each step. Nonredundancy is the objective in normalization, since uncontrolled redundancy not only leads to waste of storage but is also a breeding ground for inconsistencies where multiple copies of the same fact are not exactly the same. Inconsistency is the major threat to the usefulness of a database. It is commonly accepted that an inconsistent database is worse than no database since it misleads users into inappropriate actions or erodes their confidence in the whole systems department.

The conversion of an E-R diagram into a relational database is straightforward. Each entity and each relationship corresponds to a relation. All attributes of an entity become the attributes of the corresponding relation. All attributes of a relationship also become the attributes of the corresponding relation. Also, since each relationship is characterized by the related entities, its corresponding relation also contains as attributes the identifiers of the related entities.

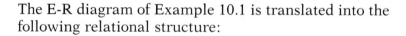

## ◆ EXAMPLE 10.2. ◆

The E-R diagram of Example 10.1 is translated into the following relational structure:

> STUDENT (id#, name, dept)
> COURSE (course#, credit)
> PROFESSOR (name, rank, dept)
> INSTRUCTOR (course#, pname)
> ENROLLMENT (course#, sid#, dept, grade)
> ADVISOR (sid#, pname)
> PREREQUISITE (course#, prereq#)

where pname and sid# are synonyms for professor's name and student's id#, respectively, and prereq# is the course# for the prerequisite course.

The normalization process is done in five steps, resulting in first, second, third, Boyce-Codd, and fourth normal forms. *First normal form* (1NF) is merely the relational structure obtained from the E-R diagram with the keys identified for each relation. The key for a relation is the set of attributes that uniquely identifies each row of that relation. The key of each relation is underlined in Example 10.2. One major assumption is that a student may be registered in multiple departments, and hence the student id# does not uniquely identify each row in the student relation, but only the (id#, dept) pair does. In general, multivalued attributes are included in the key to uniquely identify each row. Another major assumption is that each student has only one advisor, and hence pname in the **ADVISOR** relation does not have to be part of the key. In general, when a one-to-many relationship is converted to a relation, the entity on the one side does not have to participate in the key of that relation. A set of relations with their keys identified is said to be in first normal form.

The *second normal form* (2NF) identifies and eliminates a type of redundancy called nonfull functional dependency. Given the following enrollment relation:

| ENROLLMENT | (student#, | course#, | credit) |
|------------|-----------|----------|---------|
|            | 2180      | CS100    | 3       |
|            | 2180      | MIS507   | 4       |
|            | 2186      | CS100    | 3       |
|            | 2192      | CS100    | 3       |

indicating who enrolled in what courses for how many credits. Assuming that each course is offered for a fixed number of credits, the redundancy in this relation is the fact that "CS100 is a 3 credit course" is recorded three times, for each student taking CS100. There are three problems with this type of redundancy.

1. The number of credits associated with a course is recorded as many times as there are students taking that

course. The practice wastes a lot of space since there may be many students taking a course.

2.  When the number of credits assigned to a course changes, a large number of records have to be modified to reflect the change. Overlooking a single record where the credit is recorded would result in an inconsistent database.

3.  Worse yet, if there are no students taking a course, then the credit value of the course cannot be recorded, since a relational database does not allow empty fields. These three problems are called, *insertion, modification,* and *deletion anomalies* resulting from redundancy. In general, redundancy is defined as the failure to record a fact only once, but to record it either more or only zero times.

More formally, 2NF redundancies can be recognized by identifying all functions in a relation. A relation is said to have a *function* from an attribute A to an attribute B if for every element in A there is exactly one corresponding element in B. Obviously there is always a function from the key of a relation to any of its nonkey attributes. For example, in ENROLLMENT there is an obvious function from student#-course# pair to credit. However, ENROLLMENT has another function from course# to credit because of the assumption that each course is offered for a fixed credit value. This additional function is shown as

ENROLLMENT (student#, course#, credit)

and it is called a *nonfull functional dependency* since it involves a nonkey attribute (credit) being functionally dependent on a part of the key (course#), not the full key. Nonfull functional dependencies always lead to redundancies and they are said to violate the second normal form requirements. To bring the relation into second normal form, these dependencies have to be identified and eliminated. In this particular case, "credit" is the violating attribute since it is functionally dependent on part of the key. The solution is to remove the violating attribute from the relation and to form a new relation. The new relation contains not only the removed attribute, but also a copy of its identifier, i.e., the part of the key on which the violating attribute was functionally dependent. The two relations resulting from this process are

ENROLLMENT (student#, course#)
CREDIT (course#, credit)

obtained by removing the violating attribute "credit" into a new relation CREDIT, and duplicating its identifier "course#" in the new relation as the key of that relation.

The *third normal form* (3NF) is similar to the 2NF and eliminates a type of redundancy called transitive dependency. Given the following PROFESSOR relation:

PROFESSOR (name,   dept, chairman)
            SMITH   CS   GREEN
            JONES   MIS  BROWN
            DOE      MIS  BROWN
            JOHNSON MIS  BROWN

indicating the name, department, and chairman of each professor. Assuming that each department has only one chairman, the redundancy in this relation is the fact that "BROWN is the chairman of MIS department" is recorded three times, for each professor in the MIS department. Clearly, this type of redundancy has the same insertion, deletion, and modification anomalies, and should be eliminated.

3NF redundancies are different from 2NF redundancies. Clearly, the PROFESSOR relation is in the 2NF, since no non-key attribute depends on part of the key, nor could it possibly do so, because the key has only one attribute, and there is no such thing as part of the key. However, the PROFESSOR relation has a function from dept to chairman since each department has exactly one chairman. This function is shown as

PROFESSOR (<u>name</u>, dept, chairman)

and it is called a *transitive dependency* since a nonkey attribute is dependent on another nonkey attribute, and is only transitively dependent on the key. Transitive dependencies always lead to redundancies and they are said to violate the 3NF requirements. To bring the relation into 3NF, these dependencies have to be identified and eliminated. In this particular case, "chairman" is the violating attribute since it is functionally dependent on another nonkey attribute. The solution is to remove the violating attribute from the relation, and to form a new relation. The new relation contains not only the removed attribute, but also a copy of its identifier, i.e., the nonkey attribute on which it is functionally dependent. The two relations resulting from this process are

PROFESSOR (<u>name</u>, dept)
CHAIR (<u>dept</u>, chairman)

obtained by removing the violating attribute "chairman" into a new relation CHAIR, and duplicating its identifier "dept" in the new relation as the key of that relation.

The first three normal forms are the most commonly used and the most useful ones. They are also easy to remember since they deal with

1. the key
2. the whole key
3. nothing but the key.

1NF requires the identification of the key, 2NF requires that all nonkey attributes depend on the whole key (not a part of it), and 3NF requires that all nonkey attributes depend on nothing but the key.

## Higher Normal Forms

There are two more steps in normalization that are useful but not as commonly used as the first three. The violations of these higher normal forms are not very common in real life, but when they do occur they should be eliminated.

The *Boyce-Codd normal form* (BCNF) deals with relations with multiple keys. Basically, it states that when there are multiple keys, the first three steps of normalization should be repeated for every key. Given the following registration relation:

```
REG (student#, dept, advisor)
     2180      CS    SMITH
     2180      MIS   JONES
     2186      CS    SMITH
```

where a student can have multiple departments and multiple advisors, but only one advisor in each department. Advisors belong to unique departments and can only advise the students in that department. In this example, the fact that "SMITH is in the CS department" is recorded twice. Actually, the department of each advisor is recorded as many times as there are students she advises. This type of redundancy clearly exhibits all the insertion, deletion, and modification anomalies, although the relation is in 3NF, since no nonkey attribute is functionally dependent on a part of the key or another nonkey attribute.

Formally, BCNF redundancies are found in relations with multiple keys and a redundancy is merely a violation of one of first three normal forms with respect to one of the keys. The registration relation has two alternative keys and an additional function. It has no violations with respect to one key, but does have a violation of the 2NF with respect to another key as shown below.

REG (student#, dept, advisor)

The two alternative keys are the student#-dept pair, and the student#-advisor pair. Selecting student#-dept as the key leads to no violations, however selecting student#-advisor leads to a violation of the 2NF since the nonkey attribute dept is dependent on part of the key (advisor). To bring the relation into BCNF, the violating attribute dept is removed and its identifier advisor is duplicated to form a new relation, resulting in

REG (student#, advisor)

DEPT (advisor, dept)

BCNF is obtained by merely repeating the first three steps of normalization for each possible key.

Fourth normal form (4NF) is significantly different from all others since it deals with redundancies called multivalued dependencies, identified by multivalued functions. Given the following TEXT relation:

TEXT (course, professor, text)

| CS600 | Orman | Ullman |
|-------|-------|--------|
| CS600 | Conway | Date |
| CS600 | Orman | Date |
| CS600 | Conway | Ullman |

where a course can have multiple professors and also multiple texts, but all professors teaching the same course use the same textbooks in that course. In this example, CS600 has two instructors and two textbooks, and both instructors use both textbooks. Clearly, this relation is in BCNF since there are no nonkey attributes to violate any of the requirements. However, there are two sets of redundancies leading to anomalies. Each professor of a course is recorded multiple times, and also each textbook used in a course is recorded multiple times. Actually, each professor is recorded as many times as there are textbooks, and each textbook is recorded as many times as there are professors.

Formally, 4NF redundancies can be recognized by identifying all multivalued functions. A relation is said to have a

The complete process of normalization is demonstrated by the following example. Given a product relation for a retailer

PRODUCT (manufacturer, product, site, price, #employees)

which contains the manufacturer, the product name, the site of production, the price of the product by each manufacturer, and the number of employees in each site by each manufacturer. Each manufacturer can produce multiple products, each manufacturer can have multiple sites, but for a given manufacturer all products are produced on every site, i.e., there is no specialization with respect to site. The following functions follow from this description:

PRODUCT (<u>manufacturer</u>, <u>product</u>, <u>site</u>, price, #employees)

The normalization process is shown below in its detailed steps:

1NF:   PRODUCT (<u>manufacturer</u>, <u>product</u>, <u>site</u>, price, #employees)
2NF:   PRODUCT (<u>manufacturer</u>, <u>product</u>, <u>site</u>)
       PRICE (<u>manufacturer</u>, <u>product</u>, price)
       EMP (<u>manufacturer</u>, <u>site</u>, #employees)
3NF:   same
BCNF:  same
4NF:   PRODUCT (<u>manufacturer</u>, <u>product</u>)
       SITE (<u>manufacturer</u>, <u>site</u>)
       PRICE (<u>manufacturer</u>, <u>product</u>, price)
       EMP (<u>manufacturer</u>, <u>site</u>, #employees)

The relations PRODUCT and SITE can be eliminated since they are included as part of other relations, hence they are redundant, resulting in the following database:

PRICE (<u>manufacturer</u>, <u>product</u>, price)
EMP (<u>manufacturer</u>, <u>site</u>, #employees)

multivalued function from an attribute A to an attribute B, if for every element in A, the same set of elements correspond to it in B irrespective of any other attribute values. In the TEXT relation, CS600 has two professors irrespective of the textbooks, and CS600 has two textbooks irrespective of the professors. In other words, for a given course, one gets the same set of professors no matter which textbook is chosen, or the same set of textbooks no matter which professor is chosen. These two multivalued functions are shown as

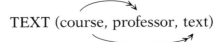

$$\text{TEXT (course, professor, text)}$$

The multivalued functions are always within the key, and they always come in pairs. To bring the relation into 4NF, these multivalued functions are eliminated by splitting the relation into two. In each case the attribute violating the 4NF requirement by being multivalued-functionally dependent on another is removed and a new relation is formed by duplicating its identifier. The resulting two relations are

PROF (<u>course, professor</u>)
TEXT (<u>course, text</u>)

It is important to remember that 4NF violations always take place within the key, and at least three attributes are necessary within the key to produce a pair of multivalued functions.

## QUESTIONS

1. Design a database for an organization of your choice using an E-R diagram and a data dictionary.

2. Convert your informal design into a relational structure and normalize to fourth normal form. Show each step.

3. Locate a relational database management system available at your computing center. Define your structure using the data definition language of your system.

4. Design 12 queries to be directed at your database, each corresponding to a query in Question 1 of Chapter 8. Make sure that the corresponding queries have exactly the same relational calculus structure (i.e., they result in the same relational calculus expression except for the names of relations and attributes). Write your queries in English and in Relational Calculus.

5. Load some fictitious data into your database. Make sure the answers to your 12 questions are all nonempty.

6. Write your queries using the calculus-based language of your system, and debug and execute them.

## BIBLIOGRAPHY

Rishe, N. *Database Design Fundamentals.* Englewood Cliffs, NJ: Prentice Hall, 1988.

Ullman, J. D. *Principles of Database Systems.* Rockville, MD: Computer Science Press, 1984.

Vetter, M., Maddison, R. N. *Database Design Methodology.* Englewood Cliffs, NJ: Prentice Hall, 1981.

♦

# Chapter 11

# Database Maintenance

Databases are not static structures. They have to be maintained to continue to be useful, relevant, up-to-date, correct, and secure. They have to be updated as the environment changes to correctly reflect the state of the world. They have to allow for the correct execution of multiple tasks accessing them concurrently. They have to recover from crashes of hardware or software. They have to provide security for sensitive data. Finally, they have to maintain the integrity of the system by protecting the data from errors and misuses. These are all services provided by the database management system and the database administrator, and these are more systems-oriented topics than the user-oriented topics of the last several chapters.

## Database Update

Database updating may involve the cooperation between a database system and a programming language. To update a data item, it has to be retrieved (a database operation); a new value should be computed (a procedure); and the new value should be stored in the database (another database operation).

The interface between a database and the programming language will be studied in Chapter 12. Except for the interface that feeds data back and forth between the two components, the update process is simple. In fact, many database management systems provide simple programming language constructs within their data languages to do simple updating without interfacing to a programming language.

◆ **EXAMPLE 11.1.** ◆

To update the savings account balance of a bank customer after a withdrawal W, the following steps are taken:

1. Retrieve account balance into variable BAL
2. Check if $BAL - W \geq$ minimum balance requirement
3. $BAL = BAL - W$
4. Store BAL as the account balance

The first and the fourth steps are database functions, and the other two steps are programming functions.

## Concurrency

A database is a shared resource, and many update operations may run concurrently. Since the database operations are much slower than central processing operations, many database transactions may share one central processing unit to keep it fully utilized, as each one spends long periods waiting for its data to arrive from secondary storage devices. Although an essential part of an efficient database environment, concurrency may also lead to serious problems. Multiple database updates running concurrently may undo each other's updates and lead to errors.

### ◆ EXAMPLE 11.2. ◆

A withdrawal and a deposit transaction running against a bank account may interfere with each other's updates as follows:

WITHDRAWAL of $100        DEPOSIT of $300.

1. Retrieve account balance $500

         2. Retrieve account balance $500

3. Check if $500 - 100 >$ minimum balance requirement
4. Compute $500 - 100 = \$400$
5. Store $400 as account balance

         6. $500 + 300 = 800$
         7. Store $800 as account balance

In this example the withdrawal transaction starts execution but interrupts while waiting for its data, and the deposit transaction takes over the central processing unit. Consequently, they both receive the same current value from the database, and the last transaction to finish the update overrides the other transaction's updates.

To solve the interference problem created by concurrency, a number of locking strategies may be used. The simplest strategy is for each transaction to lock the files it uses and prevent other transactions from accessing them until it is through. This simple strategy may lead to a serious "deadlock" problem. If two transactions need the same two files to execute, and if each acquired one and locked it, then both transactions would end up waiting for each other in a deadlock. Many algorithms have been devised to break the deadlock when it occurs, or to prevent it altogether without sacrificing the efficiency resulting from concurrency. The basis of all algorithms is communication among the concurrent transactions so that a deadlock may be detected and broken by one of the transactions.

## *Recovery*

Hardware and software failures are common in a database environment since they involve a variety of cooperating machines and their complex software. It is important to recover gracefully from crashes without sacrificing the integrity of the system. The major threat to the integrity of the system comes from crashes that interrupt transactions in the middle of execution. Since a transaction is a complete and indivisible unit of execution, it is difficult to restart it from the point where it left off and any intermediate changes it made to the database may remain and violate the integrity of the system. The most common solution is the *rollback procedure* which takes the system back to the state before the transaction started and then executes the complete transaction again. The rollback procedure requires the system to store and remember the state that existed just before the transaction started by taking a snapshot of the affected part of the database, and to restore the system to that state if a crash or an error occurs before the transaction is complete. The symmetrical strategy of *delayed commitment* works similarly. In this strategy, all effects of the transaction are recorded on a temporary copy of the relevant portion of the database. Only after the transaction is successfully completed may the temporary copy be used to replace the permanent database. At the moment of replacement the transaction is said to be "committed," and the database values are modified.

## Security

The importance of security is easily appreciated, especially when newspaper headlines are full of computer break-ins, viruses that destroy data, and national and commercial intelligence breaches. There are two general types of security threats. Those threats that result in loss of data either through physical disasters such as fire, hardware failures, or sabotage, or software errors such as erasing or overwriting data in storage devices, can be alleviated by storing secure backup copies of all data. The threat of access to data by unauthorized people is more difficult to deal with. The major tool of protection against unauthorized access is locking. Locking can be accomplished through hardware or software means and is used to block access to sensitive information. There are three types of locking: subject locking, object locking, and action locking. *Subject locking* is used to lock users out through passwords, account numbers, security codes, etc. They are designed to keep unauthorized users out of the system altogether. They are simple but effective. *Action locking* prevents certain actions from taking place. The most common example is "read only" memory which allows users to read data but prevents them from writing or updating. *Object locking* is the most sophisticated type of locking and allows a user to access certain objects but not others. The critical decision in object locking is *locking granularity*, which refers to the size of objects to be locked. Files are the most common objects to be locked. An EMPLOYEE file, for example, is not available for public viewing since it usually contains sensitive information about employees and consequently may be locked, with access restricted only to personnel managers. Sometimes individual attributes are locked. The SALARY field of the EMPLOYEE file may be locked, for example, with access restricted to managers, although the rest of the EMPLOYEE file may be open to all users. Locking individual records is expensive but sometimes essential. In an automated bank environment, it is essential that each customer has access only to his account and nobody else's. Locking individual data items is rare and very expensive. It is possible to envision a bank environment where customers have access to all of their account data except their credit rating, which would require locking just that data item for each account record.

## Integrity

Each database has a number of integrity constraints associated with it. *Integrity constraints* are logical expressions that must be true at all times. They reflect the meaning of the data in the system and act as the police force of the system by catching violating data and reporting it. Integrity constraints are critical in catching typing, interpretation, and computational errors before they correct the system and render it unusable. Some common integrity constraints have been mentioned in previous chapters. The primary keys of relations are integrity constraints that enforce the uniqueness of key values throughout the relation. Semantic data models provide standard integrity constraints such as nonoverlapping for each attribute, which enforces that attribute values are mutually exclusive. There are more general integrity constraints in a database system that require the existence of a constraint language to express them unambiguously and execute them against the database. A typical example is a constraint on an EMPLOYEE file that states that no employee earns more than his manager. In order to express this constraint, a constraint language as powerful as Predicate Logic is needed.

Catching violations is only part of the responsibility of an integrity system. It also has to find a way to clean the system. It is not always clear what steps to take to correct a violation. The system cannot merely eliminate violating data, but also has to determine the source of the problem and correct it. Some simple integrity systems merely report the violation and expect the database administrator to correct the situation manually.

More sophisticated integrity systems provide an audit trail that traces the problem to its source, whether it be a data entry error, a computational error, or a hardware failure, and help the database administrator to obtain the correct values and substitute them for the erroneous data.

## Distributed Databases

Although a database is defined as a centrally controlled reservoir of data, central control does not imply central storage of all data in one location. Organizational data may be distributed geographically while maintaining central control over consistency and lack of redundancy. Distribution is useful when the organization is geographically dispersed and data transportation costs are significant. Typical examples are large manufacturing companies with multiple sites. A number of optimization problems arise when the sites are not completely independent and need to share data. The two most common optimization problems are the selection of a site to store each data item, and the selection of transportation routes for each item needed in a nonlocal site, to minimize transportation costs. A third problem involves the execution of join operations involving two files on two different sites. The obvious solution of transporting one file to the other site to perform the join is not necessarily the most efficient solution. The concept of *semijoin* is used for this purpose, and usually leads to a more efficient solution. To join two files P(A,B,C) and Q(C,D,E) residing on two different sites, first $X = P[C]$ is transported to the second site; then the join $Y = X[C = C]Q$ is performed, and the join $Y$ which is a smaller file than Q is transported back to site 1; and finally $Y[C = C]P$ is performed to produce the final result. Also, all selections and projections are done locally before transporting files for joining to further minimize data traffic.

# QUESTIONS

1. Use predicate calculus as a constraint language to express the following integrity constraints, given the relation EMPLOYEE (name, age, dept, skill).
   a. "Name" is the key for the relation, i.e., the name value is unique for each row in the EMPLOYEE relation.
   b. No two employees in the same department have the same skill.
   c. "Dept" is a nonchangeable attribute, i.e., dept of an employee cannot be changed once entered.
   d. All employees with skill "programmer" are over 21 years of age.

2. Locate a commercial relational database management system and enter these constraints using its language.

3. Try to enter data into the system that violate these constraints. Observe the response of the system.

# BIBLIOGRAPHY

Date, C. J. *Introduction to Database Systems*. Reading, MA: Addison-Wesley Publishing Co. Inc., 1981.

Fisher, R. P. *Information Systems Security*. Englewood Cliffs, NJ: Prentice Hall, 1984.

Gallegos, F., Richardson, D. R., Borthick, A. F. *Audit and Control of Information Systems*. El Paso, TX: Southwestern, 1987.

Perry, A. *Ensuring Database Integrity*. New York: John Wiley & Sons, 1983.

Chapter 12

◆

# Database Extensions

A database is the major shared and centrally controlled component of the database application system environment. However, the database does not capture the procedures, and the procedures still have to be included in the system. There are two general approaches to incorporating the procedures into the system. *Embedded database languages* allow accessing databases from inside a programming language, and *extended database languages* allow specification of procedures within the database language itself.

## Embedded Database Languages

Embedded database language approach to the database application systems involves three major components: the database and its management system, the programs and their translators, and the interface between the database and programs. Both the database and the program components have been studied in detail in previous chapters. The interface is a complex component and it is the subject of this section. The interface allows the two components to exchange data with each other without disrupting each other's operations and without losing their independence. The database language and the programming language each have their own tasks to perform and coordinating the two while preserving their independence is a complex task. The reason for the name "embedded database language" is because the database language statements are inserted into the programming language, to be interpreted as calls to the database system from inside a program. The user interacts with the programming language, and the programming language issues data requests to the database system.

◆ **EXAMPLE 12.1.** ◆

The interface can be called from a program by using a special **INTERFACE** command that takes any database language statement as an argument and passes it on to the database management system.

```
INTERFACE('OPEN ACCOUNT TRANSACTION')
INTERFACE('FIND BALANCE<0')
INTERFACE('MAP TO TRANSACTION VIA AT')
INTERFACE('CLOSE ACCOUNT')
```

are some examples given the following network database for a bank environment:

$$AT \begin{cases} \longrightarrow \text{ACCOUNT (ANO, TYPE, BALANCE)} \\ \longrightarrow \text{TRANSACTION (TNO, AMOUNT)} \end{cases}$$

containing the account number, account type and balance of each account, and the transaction number and amount of each transaction. The relationship AT links each transaction to the account it effects.

The interface has two other major functions in addition to passing data requests and responses back and forth. The first function is declaring and naming the data returned by the database management system in a form usable by the programming language. Programming languages have different naming and data declaration conventions than databases and the interface has to accommodate those differences by appropriate conversion.

◆ **EXAMPLE 12.2.** ◆

The following statement retrieves the account number and balance of the current account record, and names them X and Y, respectively, as program variables with appropriate declarations:

INTERFACE('GET ANO BALANCE AS X Y')

The last function of the interface is to pass data from the program variables to the database management system. Typical examples are in the use of program variables in forming database queries.

◆ **EXAMPLE 12.3.** ◆

The following statement finds all accounts whose balance is less than a threshold value computed by the program and stored in variable X:

INTERFACE('FIND BALANCE<VALUE(X)')

where the expression VALUE(X) is replaced by the value of the variable X by the interface before passing the expression to the database management system.

◆ **EXAMPLE 12.4.** ◆

The following program shows a complete interface between a network database system and a programming language. Given a BANK database with the following structure:

AI AT
→ ACCOUNT (ano, type, balance)
→ TRANSACTION (tno, amount)
→ INTEREST (type, rate)

The following program prints a bank statement containing the account number, the old balance, the transaction amount, and the new balance for each account. The program assumes exactly one transaction per account and no interest.

```
PRINT 'ACCOUNT', 'OLD BALANCE',
            'TRANSACTION', 'NEW BALANCE'
INTERFACE ('OPEN, ACCOUNT TRANSACTION
                              INTEREST')
INTERFACE ('FIND ALL')
DO
  INTERFACE ('GET ANO BALANCE AS X Y')
  IF EOF EXIT
  PRINT X, Y,
  INTERFACE ('MAP TO TRANSACTION VIA AT')
  INTERFACE ('GET AMOUNT AS Z')
  W=Y+Z
  PRINT Z, W
END
```

Note that database loops are replaced by program loops and an error check which indicates the end of a file. The standard interface moves only one record at a time and all loops should be written in the programming language. For this reason, the embedded approach is more appropriate for record-at-a-time network databases. With relational systems which return a relation at a time the interface is more complicated and an extended database language approach is more appropriate.

Most major network database management systems provide an interface to standard programming languages, most commonly to COBOL, PL1, FORTRAN, BASIC, or PASCAL.

## Extended Database Languages

Extended database languages attempt to capture procedures without utilizing a programming language but completely within the database framework by merely providing additional operations. This approach is particularly effective with relational databases which provide high-level operations for data retrieval and are often incompatible with programming languages. The advantage of a relational database language to manipulate a relation-at-a-time is lost if the programming language has to consequently manipulate the retrieved data record-at-a-time. Instead, extending the database language with new relation-at-a-time operations to capture procedures leads to powerful languages completely within the database framework. The most commonly needed operations to capture procedures are arithmetic, aggregate arithmetic such as SUM and AVERAGE, and formatting for display. Looping and conditionals can be handled implicitly using the database language.

Relational Algebra can easily be extended to include arithmetic operations. Since Relational Algebra already provides the capability to identify any subset of the database and place it in one relation, an arithmetic operation that can operate on two columns to generate a third column will constitute a general arithmetic capability. $+$, $-$, $\times$, $/$ operations are provided to operate on columns of a relation and assign the result to a new column.

---

♦ **EXAMPLE 12.5.** ♦

Given the following relational database for a bank environment:

ACCOUNT (ano, type, balance, nbalance)
TRANSACTION (tno, ano, amount)

containing information about bank accounts and the transactions involving them, where nbalance is an empty field created to contain the new balance of each account. Assuming only one transaction per account, extended relational algebra can be used to compute the new balance as follows:

ACCOUNT[ano = ano']TRANSACTION
[nbalance←balance + amount] [ano, balance, nbalance]

This expression not only computes the nbalance field, but also prints a report containing account number, the old balance, and the new balance in three columns.

---

The aggregate arithmetic operators such as SUM and COUNT are also defined on columns.

---

♦ **EXAMPLE 12.6.** ♦

The average account balance is computed as follows:

SUM(ACCOUNT[balance])/COUNT(ACCOUNT[balance])

or by defining intermediate relations:

A←ACCOUNT[balance]
SUM(A)/COUNT(A)

---

The major limitation of extended relational algebra follows from the fundamental limitation of relational databases to deal only with simple relations, which are flat files. They can not accommodate nested structures which are common in database applications. For example, extending the bank example to multiple transactions would require a nested structure to list multiple transactions per account without repeating the account numbers. This structure is not permitted for arithmetic or for display purposes. Consequently, the structure has to be flattened to effectively manipulate it in this environment. For display purposes, the structure can be filled with repeated account numbers to flatten it, but for arithmetic purposes the only approach is to rotate the repeating field and list it horizontally. For that purpose, one has to know the exact number of items in the repeating field, or classify records with respect to the number of items in the repeating field. (See Question 3.)

## RDB-BASIC Interface

RDB is a DEC database management system running on all VAXs. Its interface to BASIC is similar to the stylized interface except for the use of an external **BASIC** function **RDB$INTERPRET** instead of **INTERFACE**. RDB uses INVOKE command to open a whole database with many files, START_STREAM to open a file and find all records satisfying a condition, FETCH to retrieve the current record, an END_STREAM to close a file. The following program corresponds to Example 12.4. It prints a bank statement containing a list of accounts, their old and new balances, and the transactions effecting them. It assumes exactly one transaction per account. It uses a status variable S1 which contains an integer returned by RDB$INTERPRET everytime it executes. It returns the integer 1 if it is a successful database operation; it returns an error code indicating the type of error that occurred otherwise. This program uses it to check for end-of-file condition only. S1≠1 is assumed to indicate end-of-file since no other error conditions are being considered. !VAL is a fictitious variable to facilitate the data exchange between the program and the database. It is a variable of the interface program that holds values temporarily before they are transferred. The "by desc" clause allows the description of the data item in one environment to be translated into a data declaration in the other automatically.

```
10    external integer function
      rdb$interpret
20    s1=rdb$interpret ('invoke database
      filename bank')
30    print 'account', 'old balance',
      'transactions', 'new balance'
40    s1=rdb$interpret ('start_stream st1
      using a in account')
50    s1=rdb$interpret ('fetch st1')
60    if s1<>1 then s1=rdb$interpret
      ('end_stream st1')\STOP
70    s1=rdb$interpret ('get !val=a.ano;
      !val=a.type; !val=a.balance end_get',
      x by desc, y by desc, z by desc)
80    print x, z,
90    s1=rdb$interpret ('start_stream st2
      using t in transaction with
      t.ano=!val', x by desc)
100   s1=rdb$interpret ('fetch st2')
110   s1=rdb$interpret ('get !val=t.amount
      end_get', w by desc)
120   print w, \print z+w\s1=rdb$interpret
      ('end_stream st2')\goto 50
130   end
```

RDB files can be created using the RDO command. The following commands show the creation of ACCOUNT(ano type,balance) in the bank database:

```
rdo
define database bank
define field ano datatype is signed word.
define field type datatype is text size is 2.
define field balance datatype is f-floating.

define relation account.
ano.
type.
balance.
end account relation.

store a in account using
a.ano=2118;
a.type="AZ";
a.balance=1800
end-store

commit
exit
```

To erase a record:

```
for a in account
with a.ano=2118
erase a
end-for
```

To delete a relation:

```
delete relation account.
```

## RBASE Report Writer

RBASE is a Micro Rim Inc. product based on relational algebra as introduced in Chapter 8. Its report writer is a typical

database language extension to accommodate arithmetic and display functions. The extension is similar to the stylized language of Chapter 12, except that the keyword ASSIGN TO is used to create new columns instead of the symbol ← and an extensive formatting facility is provided through a menu system. The aggregate arithmetic operators such as SUM and COUNT are provided. They are entered as separate expressions independent of relational algebra. They are assumed to be executed through an implicit loop running through the rows of the relation defining the report. Only one relation is allowed to define the report. All data needed for the report have to be compiled into one relation for the RBASE report writer.

The following program corresponds to Example 12.5. It prints a bank statement containing a list of accounts and their old and new balances. It assumes exactly one transaction per account.

```
rename ano to ano1 in transaction
join account using ano with transaction using
                      ano1 forming a where eq
assign nbalance to balance + amount in a
project b from a using ano balance nbalance
remove a
rename ano1 to ano in transaction

reports
report name: accounts
relation name: b
define
          nbalance = balance + amount
          ttotal = sum of amount
                    (to be executed for each row of the
                     relation b)
          count = count + 1
          tave = ttotal / count
edit                (to enter the report headings on the
                     screen as they should appear on the
                     report)
```

```
locate              (to enter the format of each value on
                      the report)
mark                (to mark the heading, detail, and
                      footing lines of the report)
quit                (to quit report definition)
print accounts      (to print the report)
```

RBASE relations can be created by using the **DEFINE** command of **RBASE**. The following commands show the creation of the relation ACCOUNT(ano,type,balance) in the database named bank on device c:

```
define c:bank

attributes
ano integer
type text 2
balance real

relations
account with ano type balance
end

load account
2118 AZ 1800
2126 KL 215.60
end
exit
```

## QUESTIONS

1.  Given the following network database:

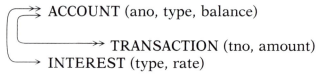

ACCOUNT (ano, type, balance)

TRANSACTION (tno, amount)

INTEREST (type, rate)

Write an embedded program to access the database and print a bank statement containing the account number, the old balance, the transaction amounts, and the new balance for each account. The new balance should be computed as

New balance = old balance + old balance × interest rate
              + Σ transaction amounts for that account

The report should consist of four columns, with multiple transactions corresponding to an account listed vertically. A final row of the report should contain the column totals for old balances, transactions, and new balances. Example 12.4 solves this problem, assuming exactly one transaction per account, no interest and no totals. Your program should relax these assumptions.

2.  Locate a commercial embedded system such as RDB-BASIC. Create the database of Question 1 in your system and load some data. Solve Question 1 using your system. Debug and execute your program.

3.  Given the following relational database:

> ACCOUNT (ano, type, balance)
> TRANSACTION (tno, ano, amount)
> INTEREST (type, rate)

write an extended relational algebra program to access the database and print a bank statement containing the account number, the old balance, and the new balance for each account. The new balance should be computed as

New balance = old balance + old balance × interest rate
              + Σ transaction amounts for that account.

The report should consist of three columns. A final row of the report should contain column totals for the old balances and the new balances. Example 12.5 solves this problem, assuming exactly one transaction per account, no interest, and no totals. Your program should relax these assumptions.

4. Locate a commercial system supporting extended relational algebra such as **RBASE** Report Writer. Create the database of Question 3 in your system and load some fictitious data. Solve Question 3 using your system. Debug and execute your program.

## BIBLIOGRAPHY

Hansen, G. W. *Database Processing with Fourth Generation Languages.* El Paso, TX: Southwestern, 1988.

Martin, J., McClure, C. *Structured Techniques for Computing.* Englewood Cliffs, NJ: Prentice Hall, 1986.

# *Part*
# *III*

◆

# *Knowledge Base Application Systems*

Knowledge base application systems are characterized by the sharing of procedures. They provide a shared reservoir of procedures, called a knowledge base, available to many applications. Applications are built by relying heavily on the procedures already available in the knowledge base, rather than from scratch. The knowledge base is managed by a software system called the *knowledge base management system,* and the manager in charge of this shared resource is called a *knowledge base administrator.*

The need for sharing procedures arises in an environment where a multitude of similar but not identical applications have to be supported. Application programs as units of procedure fail to take advantage of similarities among applications through sharing, since two programs are distinct and largely independent no matter how similar they are, unless they are identical. A centrally controlled knowledge base containing smaller components of procedure makes it possible to share procedures among applications. In an environment where many applications are slightly modified versions of each other, a shared centrally controlled knowledge base may lead to significant savings. This environment is typical of *decision support systems* and *expert systems* where a basic procedure is modified to fit the individual needs of each user or application. These personalized applications are typical in decision support systems where the decision-making process of an individual user has to be supported, or in expert systems where the expertise of an individual user is simulated. In both cases, the environment is fluid, ill structured, and even idiosyncratic, and individual differences are critically important, leading to many individualized versions of the same basic application. For this reason, decision support systems and expert systems are often designed around centrally controlled shared knowledge bases, and fall into the category of knowledge base application systems.

The major disadvantage of knowledge base application systems is the overhead associated with maintaining a central utility. The most critical component of the overhead is the cost of maintaining a large reservoir of procedures that serves the needs of all users current and prospective, and making it accessible to all who need it. The second component of the overhead is the difficulty of locating and retrieving the relevant procedures for each user from a large shared pool, and combining them in a meaningful way to build an application program. This task is considerably more difficult and costly than using a custom designed system serving only one application. The transition from a database application environment to the knowledge base application environment is justified when there is sufficient overlap among the procedural needs of applications so that the benefits from elimination of redundancy exceed the cost of overhead resulting from centralized management.

There are many tools used to capture procedures in smaller units than application programs, since small units of procedures is the critical characteristic of knowledge base application systems. Rules, frames, functions, and predicates have all been used. Rules are the oldest, most flexible, and most widely used tools to build knowledge base application systems, and Part III will concentrate on rules as procedural units.

# Chapter 13

♦

# Rules

*Rules* are simple conditionals that indicate the actions to be taken whenever certain conditions hold. The general structure is

$$c_1, \ldots, c_n \rightarrow a_1, \ldots, a_m$$

which indicates that the actions $a_1, \ldots, a_m$ are to be taken whenever the conditions $c_1, \ldots, c_n$ all hold. This structure was first invented by the French mathematician Emile Post in 1943, and its computational completeness was proved. They were originally called "Post production rules" after the inventor, but many versions developed later are referred to as "rules" in general. There are many types of rules, depending on how conditions and actions are described. Procedural statements and logical clauses are the most common choices leading to the two general types of rules as production rules and logic rules. These two types of rule-based systems are the subject of Part III after an introduction to a trivial class of rule-based systems that use arithmetic operations as actions. This class of rule-based systems is called *spreadsheets* and will be introduced in Chapter 14.

# *Sharing Rules*

Rules are small components of procedures, and a large shared reservoir of rules as a knowledge base facilitates sharing of procedures among many applications. However, sharing may take two different forms and it is important to recognize both forms. The first type of sharing involves two applications using the same rule at a given point in time without duplicating it. This is the common understanding of sharing and it is referred to as "sharing in space." "Sharing in time," on the other hand, refers to using the same rule by the two versions of the same application. Sharing in time is a more subtle type of sharing. It is usually referred to as ease of maintenance or ease of modification. However, different versions of the same application can easily be viewed as different applications, and without sharing, any minor modification requires the complete understanding of the application as a whole. The ability to modify only some rules, with no attention to the rest of the rules in an application, indicates an ability to share the unmodified rules between versions. This type of sharing in time is probably as important as the sharing in space since traditionally maintenance of procedures is considered a major source of difficulty and cost, precisely because a complete application has to be evaluated, understood, and nearly overhauled for every minor modification. Rule-base systems are extremely promising in alleviating the maintenance problem, in addition to facilitating sharing among distinct applications.

Sharing among applications also suggests a different approach to design and development. Extensive sharing among developers of applications eliminates the strong association between a developer and an application, and eliminates the need for a detailed overall design for each application. Instead, systems are put together from bits and pieces of existing information, and individual developers find themselves merely defining small bits and pieces of information for the general pool called the knowledge base. This approach to development undermines the control of analysts who are traditionally in the business of creating overall designs, and reduces their importance. Reducing the responsibilities of analysts allows other agents such as end users and the system to expand into that territory and eliminate some analyst positions. This environment is characterized by increasing direct and user-system interaction.

## QUESTIONS

1. What is a knowledge base? What are some of the tools used in knowledge bases?

2. What is a rule? What does it mean to share a rule?

## BIBLIOGRAPHY

Bonczek, R., Holsapple, C. W., Whinston, A. B. *Foundations of Decision Support Systems.* San Diego, CA: Academic Press, 1981.

Leigh, W. E., Doherty, M. E. *Decision Support and Expert Systems.* Southwestern Publishing Co., 1986.

Mockler, R. J. *Knowledge-Based Systems for Strategic Planning.* Englewood Cliffs, NJ: Prentice-Hall, 1989.

Sprague, R. H., Carlson, E. D. *Building Effective Decision Support Systems.* Englewood Cliffs, NJ: Prentice Hall, 1982.

Young, L. F. *Decision Support and Idea Processing Systems.* Dubuque, IA: Wm. C. Brown, 1989.

---
Chapter 14
---

# Spreadsheets

Spreadsheets provide a simple and very restricted example of rule-based systems. They are rarely viewed as rule-based systems because of their restrictiveness. They do not provide a complete programming environment. In particular, they lack the facilities for general procedural iteration and data management. Consequently, they are often augmented with a file management system and a general-purpose programming language. Of course, rules are capable of providing a complete programming environment as we will see in the next two chapters, but spreadsheets were designed to deal with a narrow class of problems effectively rather than being a general tool of development. The lack of data management facilities follows from the fact that spreadsheets expect all their data to be in the main memory. A separate file management system is utilized to manage the data on secondary storage and retrieve it. Consequently, giving a raise to all employees in an employee file, for example, can not be handled in one step, but rather in multiple steps executed by the file management system, the spreadsheet program, and the interface. The lack of general procedural iteration is most obvious in recursive tasks like finding the factorial of an integer through successive multiplications, or finding all ancestors of a person by repeatedly looking up parents in a parent-child file. Neither task can be done in a spreadsheet environment without manual control of the iteration. The major advantage of spreadsheets is the ease of modification and the consequent ability to ask "what if"–type questions. This capability, called "sharing in time" of rules by different versions of the same program, follows directly from the use of small and independent procedural components.

## Spreadsheet Programs

*Spreadsheet programs* consist of rules defined on tables. A *table* is a two-dimensional structure and is the only data structure in a spreadsheet environment. Each location of the table is called a *cell* and is identified by a row number and a column number. Each cell is defined by a rule and contains the value defined by the rule at that point in time. A *spreadsheet program*, then, is a table containing a rule in each cell, and a *spreadsheet* is the table of values defined by those rules. Each rule is a conditional of the type $c \rightarrow a_1, a_2$ where $c$ is a condition involving arithmetic comparison operations $<, \leq, >, \geq, =, \neq$, and $a_1, a_2$ involves arithmetic operations defined on cells. Each rule assigns a value to a cell. If $c$ is true then the value of the cell is computed by $a_1$, otherwise $a_2$ defines the cell. It is possible to have rules with no conditions, and they are called *unconditional rules*. They merely involve an arithmetic operation or simply a constant (a number or a character string) defining a cell.

The following spreadsheet program computes interest on a single bank account balance and derives the new balance:

| | A | B | C | D |
|---|---|---|---|---|
| 1 | "ACCOUNT" | "INTEREST RATE" | "BALANCE" | "NBALANCE" |
| 2 | 2118 | 0.08 | 1000 | C2>0→C2xB2,C2 |

Each row is defined by a number and each column by a letter. The cells A1–D1 are defined to contain constant character strings, and cells A2–C2 are defined to contain constant numbers. The cell D2 is the only cell containing a complete rule. It defines the cell to contain the account balance × interest rate if the balance is positive, and just the account balance otherwise. The spreadsheet defined by this spreadsheet program is shown below.

| | A | B | C | D |
|---|---|---|---|---|
| 1 | "ACCOUNT" | "INTEREST RATE" | "BALANCE" | "NBALANCE" |
| 2 | 2118 | 0.08 | 1000 | 1080 |

Any change in the program will automatically change the corresponding spreadsheet. For example, changing the interest rate in this program to 0.09 will change both the interest rate and the new balance in the spreadsheet. The difference between the program that defines the spreadsheet and the spreadsheet itself is subtle but critical to understanding.

Spreadsheet programs also provide aggregate arithmetic operations such as SUM, AVERAGE, MAXIMUM, and MINIMUM. They define a cell in terms of other cells.

◆ **EXAMPLE 14.2.** ◆

Given a file of bank accounts ACCOUNT (ano, type, balance) with 3 columns and 1,000 rows residing on cells A1–C1000, the following program computes the total of all account balances and prints it as the last row:

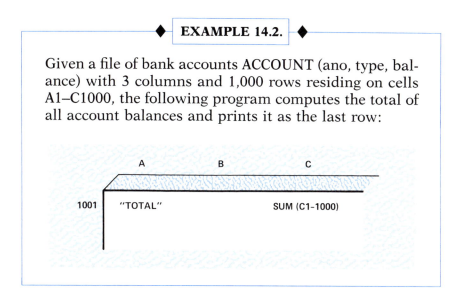

| | A | B | C |
|---|---|---|---|
| 1001 | "TOTAL" | | SUM (C1-1000) |

## Rule Clusters

A large spreadsheet program may contain thousands of cells and defining each cell separately with an independent rule is a tedious task. Spreadsheet systems provide commands that define large clusters of rules in a single step. These commands do not add significantly to the conceptual famework, but without them spreadsheet programming would be prohibitively cumbersome. The simplest of all cluster commands is the copy command which assigns the same rule to a cluster of cells.

$$\begin{pmatrix} A & 1 \\ & | \\ A10 \end{pmatrix} \leftarrow 0$$

will assign the value zero to all cells between A1 and A10.

$$\begin{pmatrix} A & 1 \\ & | \\ A10 \end{pmatrix} \leftarrow B1 + C1$$

will assign the rule $B1 + C1$ to all ten cells.

$$\begin{pmatrix} A & 1 \\ & | \\ A10 \end{pmatrix} \leftarrow \begin{pmatrix} B & 1 \\ & | \\ B10 \end{pmatrix} + \begin{pmatrix} C & 1 \\ & | \\ C10 \end{pmatrix} + 2$$

will assign the rule $B_i + C_i + 2$ to the cell $A_i$ for each i between 1 and 10.

The second class of cluster rules called **QUERY** commands are conditional cluster rules. They assign the same rule to a cluster of cells satisfying certain conditions.

Given a bank account file ACCOUNT (ano, type, balance) residing on cells A1–C1000 in three columns, the following rule lists the accounts with a negative balance starting at cell E1:

|  | A | B | C | D | E |
|---|---|---|---|---|---|
| 1 |  |  |  | $\begin{pmatrix} C & 1 \\ & \| \\ C1000 \end{pmatrix}<0 \rightarrow$ | $\begin{pmatrix} A & 1 \\ & \| \\ A1000 \end{pmatrix}$ |

The third class of cluster rules called **TABLE** commands are used to classify rules with respect to a condition and list them in a table.

◆ **EXAMPLE 14.5.** ◆

Given the same ACCOUNT file residing on cells A1–C1000, and a list of account types on cells E1–E10, the following rule finds all accounts of each type and sums their balances, printing the total balance for each type of account on F1–F10.

$$
\begin{array}{l}
\quad\quad F \\
1 \quad \begin{pmatrix} E1 \\ | \\ E10 \end{pmatrix} = (B1\text{–}B1000) \rightarrow \text{SUM}(C1\text{–}C1000)
\end{array}
$$

A two-dimensional table classifying accounts with respect to type and balance, and printing total balances for each group can be created similarly if E2–E10 contains possible types, and F1–Z1 contains possible balances.

$$
\begin{array}{l}
\quad\quad F \\
2 \quad \begin{pmatrix} E2 \\ | \\ E10 \end{pmatrix} = (B1\text{-}B1000), \begin{pmatrix} F1 \\ | \\ Z1 \end{pmatrix} = (C1\text{-}C1000) \rightarrow \text{SUM}(C1\text{-}C1000)
\end{array}
$$

◆ **EXAMPLE 14.6.** ◆

Given an ACCOUNT (ano, type, balance) file residing on A1–C1000, and a TRANSACTION (tno, ano, amount) file residing on G1–I1000, compute the new balance for each account assuming exactly one transaction per account. Both files are sorted with respect to ano. The new

**EXAMPLE 14.6.** (*Continued*)

balances should be added to the account file as a new column on D1–D1000.

D

$$1 \quad \begin{pmatrix} C1 \\ | \\ C1000 \end{pmatrix} + \begin{pmatrix} I1 \\ | \\ I1000 \end{pmatrix}$$

---

## Lotus

---

LOTUS is a spreadsheet system available on many microcomputers. It is similar to the stylized spreadsheet system except for syntactic differences, especially in clustered rules. The conditional rule $c \rightarrow a_1,a_2$ is expressed as @1F($c,a_1,a_2$). All aggregate commands start with the symbol @ such as @SUM or @MAXIMUM. Copy commands are implemented by defining one cell and copying it with a @COPY command.

$$\begin{pmatrix} A \ 1 \\ | \\ A10 \end{pmatrix} \leftarrow 0$$

is expressed as

$$A1 \leftarrow 0$$

and

$$@COPY \ (A1,A2.A10)$$

to copy A1 to cells A2–A10.

$$\begin{pmatrix} A \ 1 \\ | \\ A10 \end{pmatrix} \leftarrow B1+C1$$

is expressed as

$$A1 \leftarrow \$B\$1 + \$C\$1$$
$$@COPY\ (A1,A2.A10)$$

The dollar signs are used to fix the variable name and prevent it from being indexed. Without them, A2 would be defined as $B2 + C2$, and A3 as $B3 + C3$, etc.

Finally,

$$\begin{pmatrix} A\ 1 \\ | \\ A10 \end{pmatrix} \leftarrow \begin{pmatrix} B\ 1 \\ | \\ B10 \end{pmatrix} + \begin{pmatrix} C\ 1 \\ | \\ C10 \end{pmatrix} + 2$$

is expressed as

$$A1 \leftarrow B1 + C1 + 2$$
$$@COPY\ (A1,\ A2.A10)$$

Query commands are more complicated in LOTUS, involving three components. *Input range* defines a file, *criterion range* defines the criteria of selection, and *output range* defines where to place the selected items. Given an ACCOUNT (ano, type, balance) file residing on cells A1–C1000, the following program retrieving the accounts with negative balances into cells E1–E1000:

$$1 \quad \begin{pmatrix} E \\ C1 \\ | \\ C1000 \end{pmatrix} < 0 \rightarrow \begin{pmatrix} A1 \\ | \\ A1000 \end{pmatrix}$$

is expressed in LOTUS as

```
/DATA QUERY                                    H
Input Range: A0. C1000          1      balance
Criterion Range: H1.H2          2         <0
Output Range: E1.E1000
EXTRACT
QUIT
```

It is also necessary in LOTUS that cells A0, B0, and C0 of the
ACCOUNT file contain the field names "ano", "type", and "balance", so the file actually starts at A1.

There are two separate TABLE commands in LOTUS for
one- and two-dimensional tables. The DATA TABLE 1 command has three components. "Range" defines the area allocated to the table, "input cell" defines the classification criterion, and "DSUM" is the aggregate data sum function that
specifies the file to be classified. DSUM also has three arguments: the file to be partitioned, the column to be partitioned,
and the partition criterion. Given the same ACCOUNT file as
above, and a list of account types on cells E1–E10, the following program finding the total account balances for each type:

$$1 \quad \begin{pmatrix} E1 \\ | \\ E10 \end{pmatrix} = B1-B1000 \quad \rightarrow \quad SUM(C1-C1000)$$

is expressed in LOTUS as

```
/DATA TABLE 1
Range: E0-F10       F                              H
Input cell:H1  0  @DSUM(A0.C1000,2,H0.H1)  type
               1
```

where H1 is blank and it is assumed to contain the type values
from file A0.C1000 one at a time. Argument value 2 indicates
that the column to be partitioned is the third column (2 + the
default column 1) which contains the account balances. H0.H1
indicates the location of the partition criterion, which is a list
of type values. For each type value listed in E1–E10, all accounts with that type value are retrieved from A0.C1000 file,
its third column values are totaled, and the results are entered
into F1.F10. Two-dimensional tables are created in the same
way except that the command is /DATA TABLE 2 and there
are two input cells, "Input Cell 1" corresponding to rows and
"Input Cell 2" corresponding to columns.

# QUESTIONS

1. Given the files ACCOUNT (account number, account type, balance) residing on A1–C1000, TRANSACTION (transaction number, account number, amount) residing on G1–I100, and INTEREST (account type, interest rate) residing on J1–K10, write a spreadsheet program to compute the new balance for each account as a new column D1–D1000. The new balance should be computed as

   New balance = old balance + old balance × interest rate
   $$+ \ \Sigma \ \text{transaction amounts for that account}$$

   A final row added to the ACCOUNT file should contain the column totals for the old balances and the new balances. Example 14.6 solves this problem assuming exactly one transaction per account, no interest, and no totals. Your program should relax these assumptions.

2. Locate a commercial spreadsheet system available in your computing center (such as LOTUS). Define the files of Question 1 using your system and load some fictitious data. Solve Question 1 using your system.

# BIBLIOGRAPHY

Holt, J. A. *Cases and Applications in Lotus 1-2-3.* Homewood, IL: Richard D. Irwin Inc., 1986.

Kroenke, D. M., Dolan, K. A. *Business Computer Systems.* Santa Cruz, CA: Mitchell Publishing Inc., 1987.

# Chapter 15

♦

# Production Rules

A production rule has the general structure of $c_1, \ldots,$ $c_n \rightarrow a_1, \ldots, a_m$ where $c_i$ are conditions and $a_i$ are actions. It states that whenever the conditions $c_1, \ldots, c_n$ are satisfied by the data, then the actions $a_1, \ldots, a_m$ are to be taken. All data are captured in files denoted by $F(A_1, \ldots, A_p)$ where F is a file name and $A_i$ are attributes. A production rule environment consists of production rules and files. Each rule and each file is independent of all others, with no relationships explicitly defined, satisfying the requirement of small independent components. Each condition is either in the form of $F(a_1, \ldots, a_p)$ where each $a_i$ is a constant or a variable, or in the form of $a_i \theta a_j$ where $a_i$ and $a_j$ are either constants or variables and $\theta$ is a comparison operator $<, \leq, >, \geq, =, \neq$. The condition $F(a_1, \ldots, a_p)$ is satisfied by every record in F that matches $a_1, \ldots, a_p$. $a_i \theta a_j$ is satisfied if the condition $a_i \theta a_j$ holds.

♦ **EXAMPLE 15.1.** ♦

Given the file ACCOUNT(ano, type, balance), the condition ACCOUNT($x$,1,$z$) will be satisfied by all account records with type 1, as long as $x$ and $z$ are not restricted by another condition of the rule. ACCOUNT $(x, 1, z), z<0$

pair will be satisfied by all account records of type 1 with a negative balance. Obviously, a record is said to satisfy a condition if it matches all the constants, and is able to assign its values to the variables of the condition without violating any condition. $x$ and $z$ in this example will be assigned ano and balance values of an account record, each time a record of type 1 and negative balance is found. This process is called *binding* the variables of the condition. The value bound to each variable can be used in the actions, relating the conditions to the actions of each rule.

There are five general actions in a production rule environment: insert $\downarrow$ and delete $\uparrow$ are used to insert and delete records in files; modify $\rotatebox{90}{$\curvearrowright$}$ is used to modify existing records; compute $=$ is used to do arithmetic; and print is used to print out values.

◆ **EXAMPLE 15.2.** ◆

Given the file ACCOUNT (ano, rate, balance) containing the account number, the interest rate for that account, and the account balance; the new balance of each account is computed and the file is updated as follows:

$$\text{ACCOUNT(ano,rate,bal)} \rightarrow nb = bal + bal \times rate,$$
$$\rotatebox{90}{$\curvearrowright$}\,\text{ACCOUNT(ano,rate,nb)}$$

This rule will be executed for every account record since there are no restrictions on field values. For each record, the new balance will be computed as nb, and the account record will be modified by replacing the balance field with nb.

It is important to point out that each rule defines an implicit loop. In this example, the rule is executed for each record in the ACCOUNT file. The records that satisfy the conditions of a rule are said to "trigger" the rule, and the rule is said to "fire" for each one of those records. The terminology comes from neurobiology where neurons in a human brain are said to fire by discharging their electrical content as electrical pulses, whenever their input pulses produce enough energy to exceed a threshold value. It is critical that a rule fires for every record that satisfies the conditions, and fires only once for each such record. To accomplish this task, each record that triggers a rule is tagged temporarily to prevent the same record triggering the same rule again, and the process continues until no more rules can fire. The strategy of preventing a rule being triggered by the same record repetitively is called "refraction." The terminology, again taken from neurobiology, refers to the inability of a neuron to fire repeatedly without being energy replenished during a refraction period after a firing.

---

◆ **EXAMPLE 15.3.** ◆

Given the same ACCOUNT(ano,rate,balance) file, the following rule prints all accounts with a negative balance:

ACCOUNT(ano,rate,bal), bal$<$0 $\rightarrow$ print(ano,rate,bal)

---

◆ **EXAMPLE 15.4.** ◆

Given the file ACCOUNT(ano,type,balance), the following rules create a new file SUM(type,total) containing the total balance for each type of accounts. The new file is created by first inserting a record for each type with total zero, and then updating the total field by aggregating the balances of all accounts of that type.

ACCOUNT(ano,type,bal) → ↓ SUM(type,0)
ACCOUNT(ano,type,bal), SUM(type,x) →
$$y = x + bal, \; \curlywedge SUM(type, y)$$

The first rule creates the SUM file, and the second rule repeatedly updates it until the correct totals are computed. The second rule requires the existence of an ACCOUNT record, and a corresponding SUM record to fire. Any pair of ACCOUNT-SUM records will fire the rule as long as the second field of ACCOUNT has the same value as the first field of SUM since they correspond to the same variable type. This operation is equivalent to a join of relational databases in effect. The rule is fired for all such pairs, and refraction now works on pairs preventing the same pair triggering the same rule more than once.

◆ **EXAMPLE 15.5.** ◆

Given the file ACCOUNT(ano,balance,sequence) containing account numbers, balances, and arbitrary sequence numbers, the following program will sort the file with respect to the ascending order of account numbers by rearranging the sequence numbers so that they correspond to the sequence of account numbers. The sequence field can be assumed to initially contain integers corresponding to the sequence of creation of account records, i.e., the first account opened containing 1, the second 2, etc. To sort the file, the following rule compares every record to every other record, and if the sequence numbers are found to be in the wrong order with respect to account numbers, the sequence numbers of the two records are exchanged. The two records are

**EXAMPLE 15.5.** (*Continued*)

identified by the predicates ACCOUNT and ACCOUNT′ which can be viewed as two copies of the same file.

ACCOUNT(ano,bal,seq), ACCOUNT′(ano′,bal′,seq′),
ano<ano′,seq>seq′ → ⌐ACCOUNT(ano,bal,seq′),
⌐ACCOUNT′(ano′,bal′,seq)

This is clearly not the most efficient sort algorithm. A good rule base management system is expected to do some optimization by rearranging the rules, and the order in which they fire. Production rules do very little optimization. Logic rules, discussed in Chapter 16, accomplish much more in this area.

A major disadvantage of production rule systems is the difficulty of sequencing rules. The rules are independent of each other, and to force them to fire in a particular order requires an explicit mechanism. The need to fire the rules in a particular order arises in same computations, and especially in printing reports. The most common method to sequence rules is by creating a SEQUENCE file with only one field and only one record. A file SEQUENCE (step) is used where at each step rule i fires only if the step value is i, and the rule resets the step value to i + 1 to trigger the next rule.

◆ **EXAMPLE 15.6.** ◆

Given the files ACCOUNT(ano,type,balance) and SEQUENCE (step), the following rules print the account records for the accounts 1118 and 1121, in that order, assuming SEQUENCE has been initialized to one record with step value 1:

SEQUENCE(1), ACCOUNT(1118,y,2) →
                    print(1118,y,2), SEQUENCE(2)
SEQUENCE(2), ACCOUNT(1121,y,2) → print(1121,y,2)

A more complicated sequencing requires a rule to fire for each record in a file, before the next rule is activated. This type of sequencing is accomplished by removing the records as they are used, and then testing for the nonexistence of any records left, as a condition of the next rule. Testing for nonexistence requires a negative condition.

◆ **EXAMPLE 15.7.** ◆

Given the file ACCOUNT(ano,type,balance), the following rule prints all account records with negative balances first, and then prints all account records with positive balances:

ACCOUNT(ano,type,bal), bal<0 →
                    print(ano,type,bal), ↑ACCOUNT
ACCOUNT(ano,type,bal), −ACCOUNT(ano1,type1,bal1),
                    bal1<0 → print(ano,type,bal)

where −ACCOUNT(ano1,type1,bal1) checks for nonexistence of an account record ACCOUNT(ano1, type1,bal1).

◆ **EXAMPLE 15.8.** ◆

Given the files ACCOUNT(ano,type,balance), TRANSACTION(tno,ano,amount), and SEQUENCE(step) the following rules update the account balances and print a report containing the account number and new balance for each account. The rules assume that

**EXAMPLE 15.8.** (*Continued*)

SEQUENCE is initialized to one record with value 1, and there is exactly one transaction per account.

SEQUENCE(1) → print("account number",
                          "new balance"), SEQUENCE(2)
SEQUENCE(2), ACCOUNT(ano,type,balance),
TRANSACTION(tno,ano,amount) →
nb = balance + amount, ⌐ACCOUNT(ano,type,nb),
                                          print(ano,nb)

---

## OPS5

---

OPS5, Official Production System Version 5, is a production rule base management system which is widely available on many DEC products and in many UNIX environments. It runs on top of the programming language LISP. It is similar to the standard production rule notation with minor syntactic differences. The only major difference is its difficulty with refraction when modification of records is involved. When a record is modified OPS5 views it as a new record and refraction does not apply. Consequently, the modified record may trigger the same rule again, possibly leading to an infinite loop. In OPS5, the modifications have to be treated with care, and the modified records should be tagged or removed to prevent repeated triggers. Example 15.2, for instance, when run in OPS5 will lead to an infinite loop since each time an account record is modified it will be viewed as a new account record and will be allowed to trigger the rule again. To prevent the infinite loop a common technique is to tag the account records when they are updated. A new field "status" is created for that purpose and initialized to 0. Given the file ACCOUNT (ano,rate,balance,status) the computation of the new balance is accomplished as follows:

ACCOUNT(ano,rate,bal,0) → nb = bal + bal × rate,
                                          ACCOUNT(ano,rate,nb,1)

The modification of the status field prevents a repeated trigger of the rule by any account record. All other differences are syntactic where each production rule is uniquely named, each condition or action is placed on a separate line with enclosing parentheses, records are named when they satisfy a condition, ↓ corresponds to the keyword "make", ↑ to "remove", ⊃ to "modify", = to "bind" and "compute", and print to "write". The following rules demonstrate the syntax of OPS5 by solving Example 15.8:

```
(p h
{(sequence ^step 1) ⟨seq⟩}
→
(write (crlf) account number (tab to 20) new balance)
(modify ⟨seq⟩ ^step 2))

(p d
{(sequence ^step 2) ⟨seq⟩}
{(account ^ano ⟨a⟩ ^balance ⟨b⟩) ⟨acc⟩}
{(transaction ^ano ⟨a⟩ ^amount ⟨q⟩) ⟨tr⟩}
→
(bind ⟨nb⟩ (compute ⟨b⟩ + ⟨q⟩)))
(modify ⟨acc⟩ ^balance ⟨nb⟩)
(write ⟨crlf⟩ ⟨a⟩ (tab to 20) ⟨nb⟩)
(remove ⟨tr⟩)))
```

The two rules named "h" for header and "d" for detail correspond to the two rules of Example 15.8. The first rule fires first. It moves to a new line since (crlf) stands for "carriage return-line feed", and prints the heading "account number" and then moves to column 20 to print the heading "new balance". The second rule fires for each account transaction pair with matching ano values. The matching pair are named "acc" and "tr", respectively. For each matching pair the new balance is computed, and the balance field of the account record "acc" is modified. Finally, the account number and the new balance are printed, and the transaction tr is removed. The last step is critical, since if tr is not removed it will match the same account again leading to an infinite loop. Matching to the same account is not prevented by refraction since OPS5 treats modified records as new records.

Creation of files in OPS5 is straightforward. First a file description is entered using the command "literalize" and then records are entered one at a time with a "make" command. The following rules show the creation of the files for Example 15.8:

(literalize account ano type balance)
(literalize transaction ano amount)
(literalize sequence step)
(startup)
(watch 0)
(make account ^ano 2118 ^type 1 ^balance 1800)
(make account ^ano 2126 ^type 2 ^balance 300)
(make account ^ano 2135 ^type 3 ^balance − 42000)
(make account ^ano 2142 ^type 2 ^balance 450)
(make transaction ^ano 2126 ^amount − 350)
(make transaction ^ano 2126 ^amount − 26)
(make transaction ^ano 2126 ^amount 200)
(make transaction ^ano 2135 ^amount 240)
(make transaction ^ano 2142 ^amount − 400)
(make sequence ^step 1))

## QUESTIONS

1. A portfolio database contains the following files:

   - ACCOUNT(ano,type,balance) containing the account numbers, account type, and account balance for each account in the portfolio of a customer
   - INTEREST(type,frate,crate) containing the type of account, the expected future interest rate, and the current interest rate for that type of account.

   Write production rules to create the file TRANSACTION (ano,amount) where each transaction indicates a movement of funds into an account ano. A negative amount indicates a movement of funds out of the account ano. Transactions come in pairs since each movement takes equal amount of funds from one account and deposits it into another. The amount of funds transferred from account 1 to account 2 is given by the following formula:

$$((frate2 - crate2) - (frate1 - crate1)) \times (balance1 + balance2)$$

2. Given the files ACCOUNT(ano,type,balance), TRANSACTION(ano,amount) as described in Question 1, and the file SEQUENCE(step) initialized to one record with step 1, to order the rules; write production rules to print a portfolio statement containing the account number and the new balance for each account. A similar example was given in Example 15.8. This example assumes only one transaction per customer. Your rules should relax this assumption.

3. Locate a commercial production rule base management system, such as OPS5, in your computing center. Identify the differences between your system and the standard notation used in this chapter. Load ACCOUNT, INTEREST, and SEQUENCE files into your system with fictitious data.

4. Repeat Questions 1 and 2 for your system.

# BIBLIOGRAPHY

Buchanan, B. G., Shortliffe, E. H. *Rule Based Expert Systems.* Reading, MA: Addison-Wesley, 1984.

Davis, R., Lenat, D. B. *Knowledge Based Systems in Artificial Intelligence.* New York: McGraw-Hill, 1983.

Frost, R. *Introduction to Knowledge Base Systems.* New York: Macmillan, 1986.

Harmon, P., King, D. *Expert Systems.* New York: John Wiley & Sons, 1985.

Hayes-Roth, F. *Building Expert Systems.* Reading, MA: Addison-Wesley, 1983.

# Chapter 16

◆

# Logic Rules

*Logic rules* are based on the clausal form of first-order logic, and they are also called *clausal rules* or *logic programs*. The general structure of a logic rule is $c_1, \ldots, c_n \to a_1, \ldots a_m$ where all $c_1, \ldots, c_n$ and $a_1, \ldots, a_m$ are conditions. Unlike production rules, there is no distinction between conditions and actions. Expressing both the left-hand side and the right-hand side of a rule in terms of conditions brings the rules into the realm of logic, since actions are not logical constructs, but conditions are. A logic rule is interpreted as an implication in first-order logic where if the conditions on the left are all satisfied then at least one of the conditions on the right should be satisfied. In other words, the conditions on the left are assumed to be separated by AND operators, but the conditions on the right are separated by implicit OR operators. All data are captured in files characterized by $F(A_1, \ldots, A_p)$ where F is a file name and $A_1, \ldots, A_p$ are its attributes. Each condition is either of the type $F(a_1, \ldots, a_p)$ or of the type $a_i \theta a_j$ where F is a file name; $a_1, \ldots, a_p, a_i, a_j$ are constants, variables, or functions; and $\theta$ is one of $<, \leq, >, \geq, =, \neq$. A condition $F(a_1, \ldots, a_p)$ is satisfied by every record in F that matches the arguments $a_1, \ldots, a_p$. The arguments are matched by assigning values to each variable and insuring that none of the conditions are violated. This process of assigning values to each variable without violating any of the conditions is called *instantiation*. Each possible instantiation of the left-hand side requires that at least one right-hand side condition should hold for that instantiation. For most of this chapter, we will restrict ourselves to rules with only one condition on the right. These special types of rules are called *Horn clauses*. They are very useful and much easier to manipulate and interpret than general clausal rules.

♦ **EXAMPLE 16.1.** ♦

Given the file ACCOUNT(ano,type, balance), the condition ACCOUNT($x$,1,$z$) will be satisfied by all account records with type 1, as long as $x$ and $z$ are not restricted by another condition of the rule. ACCOUNT($x$,1,$z$),$z<0$ pair will be satisfied by all account records of type 1 with a negative balance. ACCOUNT($x$,1,$z$) $\rightarrow z<0$ will require all accounts with type 1 to have a negative balance. Obviously, logic rules are implications in first-order logic where all variables are assumed to be universally quantified. For example, the rule ACCOUNT($x$,1,$z$) $\rightarrow z<0$ is equivalent to the logical statement $\forall x \ \forall z$ ACCOUNT($x$,1,$z$) $\rightarrow z<0$ which states that for every $x$ and for every $z$ in the universe, if ($x$,1,$z$) is a record in the ACCOUNT file then $z$ is negative. To remain completely within the realm of logic, the files are interpreted as predicates that map their arguments to TRUE or FALSE. The ACCOUNT file, for example, is a three-argument predicate that returns TRUE or FALSE for every possible three arguments. ACCOUNT($x$,$y$,$z$) is assumed to be TRUE if $x$,$y$,$z$ is an account record, otherwise it is assumed to be false.

Expressing all rules as logical statements has many advantages, since logic has well-understood and formally defined semantics. The most significant advantage is the ability to derive new rules from the existing rules using logical derivation methods. Such a capability is unprecedented in the computing world, and opens up the possibility of "creative" work for machines that is usually reserved for humans. Creating new information from existing information is the cornerstone of intelligent human behavior and logic rules move automated systems closer to that higher mode of operation. Logic rules also have many disadvantages. The inability to specify the explicit actions to be taken by the system requires an indirect specification of the consequences of those actions. This is a higher level of specification and leaves the system responsible for picking the right actions to achieve the desired consequences. Such systems require more sophisticated implementation and management. Moreover, the inability to specify explicit actions such as "delete" and "modify" requires roundabout specifications when deletion or modification is exactly what the task requires.

◆ **EXAMPLE 16.2.** ◆

Given the file ACCOUNT(ano,rate,balance) containing the account number, the interest rate for that account, and the account balance, the new balance of each account is computed and the file is updated by creating a new account file NACCOUNT as follows:

$$\text{ACCOUNT(ano,rate,bal), } nb = bal + bal \times rate \rightarrow$$
$$\text{NACCOUNT(ano,rate,nb)}$$

Note that the logical interpretation of this rule is the implication $\forall$ano $\forall$rate $\forall$bal $\forall$nb ACCOUNT(ano,rate, bal)$\wedge$nb $= bal + bal \times rate \rightarrow$ NACCOUNT(ano,rate,nb). Since NACCOUNT does not exist this rule requires the creation of appropriate NACCOUNT records to satisfy this logical statement. Conceptually, this logic rule triggers a series of insert actions to create NACCOUNT records until the condition is satisfied. In actuality, the NACCOUNT file does not physically exist, but it is generated only when needed. The distinction between physically existing files and files defined by rules is critical in a logic rule environment. Physically existing files are referred to as *extensional files* and they are created and maintained explicitly by a file management system. Files defined by rules are called *intensional files* and they exist only in the mind of the user. Their contents are defined by rules, determined by the contents of the extensional files, and derived only as needed. NACCOUNT above is an intensional file. Intensional files, by virtue of their virtual existence, are not bound by many of the restrictions that apply to extensional files. For example, intensional files can be defined recursively, i.e., in terms of themselves, some of their records defining other records of the same file; and they may even be infinitely large, a property that can never be possessed by an extensional file that physically exists. Given the file ACCOUNT (ano,rate,balance), the updating of the file at each time period can be done without creating a new NACCOUNT file at every period, but by time-stamping account records using a time attribute in the file

NACCOUNT(ano,rate,balance,time):
ACCOUNT(ano,rate,bal) → NACCOUNT(ano,rate,bal,0)
NACCOUNT(ano,rate,bal,t), nb = bal + bal × rate,
$$s = t + 1 \rightarrow NACCOUNT(ano,rate,nb,s)$$

Initial account records of the extensional file ACCOUNT are copied into the NACCOUNT file with time value 0, and for subsequent time periods the NACCOUNT file is merely expanded to contain the corresponding account records. It is important to note that the NACCOUNT file is infinitely large, containing account records for each time period into the indefinite future, and obviously it can not and does not physically exist in its totality. It is very different from the ACCOUNT file which only contains the initial values of each account. It is also important to note that NACCOUNT is defined recursively

**EXAMPLE 16.2.** (*Continued*)

in the second rule, i.e., some of its records are defined in terms of other records in the same file. Recursion is the cornerstone of logic rules and the only tool to create infinitely large files. Clearly, with the existence of infinitely large files, logic rules can not be allowed to fire for all data that match their left-hand sides. Rather, they should be interpreted as logical statements that must hold true for the correct data, and the derivation of intensional data should be goal directed. For example, to determine the account balances at time period 10, the derivation of the NACCOUNT file must be controlled, and the creation of new records must be halted at period 10. The strategies used by rule base management systems to accomplish this task will be studied in Chapter 17.

◆ **EXAMPLE 16.3.** ◆

Logic rules do not provide input-output commands, but leave those tasks to their file management systems. Given the ACCOUNT(ano,rate,balance) file, the following rule places all accounts with a negative balance into a special **REPORT** file to be printed by the file management system:

ACCOUNT(ano,rate,bal), bal<0 →
REPORT(ano,rate,bal)

In addition to constants and variables, logic rules utilize functions as arguments. A *function* is a mapping that returns a single value for each value of its arguments. A function S(type) associates a single value for each value of the variable type in the following example. Logic rules also rely on standard functions such as SUM, AVERAGE, MAXIMUM, MINIMUM, etc. to accomplish aggregate operations.

◆ **EXAMPLE 16.4.** ◆

Given the file ACCOUNT(ano,type,balance), the following rules create a new file TOTAL(type,total) containing the total balance for each type of accounts:

ACCOUNT(ano,type,bal), S(type) = SUM(bal) →
$$\text{TOTAL(type,S(type))}$$

where S(type) is a function containing sum of all the balances corresponding to each value of type. Each instantiation of the left-hand side updates the S(type) function by using the SUM function. Other functions such as **MAXIMUM** operate in a similar fashion. S(type) = MAXIMUM(bal), for example, would assign the largest account balance within each type to the function S(type). Functions are denoted by capital letters, and functions without arguments denote constants.

 ◆ **EXAMPLE 16.5.** ◆

Given the file ACCOUNT(ano,balance,sequence) containing account numbers, balances, and arbitrary sequence numbers, the following rules will sort the file with respect to the ascending order of account numbers by rearranging the sequence numbers so that they correspond to the sequence of account numbers. The new sorted file is created under the name SACCOUNT. Unlike production rules, logic rules cannot specify the actions to be taken to sort the file, but they describe what it means to be sorted and restrict the SACCOUNT file to be a sorted file. The actions to be taken to satisfy that restriction are determined by the system, by picking one of the many possible algorithms to achieve the desired

**EXAMPLE 16.5.** (*Continued*)

state. The following rules also demonstrate the use of arbitrary functions through a sort example:

SACCOUNT(ano,bal,seq), SACCOUNT(ano1,bal1,seq1),
ano<ano1 → seq<seq1
ACCOUNT(ano,bal,seq) → SACCOUNT(A(seq),B(seq),seq)
ACCOUNT(ano,bal,seq) → SACCOUNT(ano,bal,S(ano,bal))

The first rule establishes SACCOUNT as a sorted file with respect to ano. The remaining two rules insure that SACCOUNT contains the same records and sequence numbers as ACCOUNT. The second rule insures that SACCOUNT has the same sequence values as the ACCOUNT file, otherwise there would be no guarantee that SACCOUNT would use consecutive integers as sequence values. The third rule insures that the same ACCOUNT records also appear in the SACCOUNT file. These two rules use arbitrary functions A, B, and S to denote irrelevant arguments. The second rule states that there is an SACCOUNT record with seq as its sequence value, and some ano and balance value denoted by A(seq), and B(seq), respectively. A(seq) and B(seq) have seq as arguments since they are expected to return different ano and balance values for each sequence. Using functions A and B without arguments would require the existence of unique ano and balance values to appear with each sequence value in SACCOUNT. Similarly, the third rule asserts the existence of a record in SACCOUNT with ano, bal, and some arbitrary sequence value S(ano,bal), which is potentially different for each ano,bal pair. An example of this type shows the true nonprocedural nature of logic rules where a description of the desired outcome replaces the specification of the steps to achieve that outcome. Taken literally, the three rules above do not limit SACCOUNT only to the ACCOUNT records since implication in the opposite direction is not given. SACCOUNT may have many other records as long as they are sorted. This possibility is excluded by using a "minimality" assumption which requires the intensional files to contain the minimal set of records without violating the conditions.

◆ **EXAMPLE 16.6.** ◆

Printing reports in a particular sequence requires a number of records in the logic rule environment. Given the file ACCOUNT(ano,type,balance), to print the account records for the accounts 1118 and 1121 in that order, a line-numbered report file REPORTL (sequence,ano,type,balance) is created:

$$\text{ACCOUNT}(1118,y,z) \rightarrow \text{REPORTL}(1,1118,y,z)$$
$$\text{ACCOUNT}(1121,y,z) \rightarrow \text{REPORTL}(2,1121,y,z)$$

◆ **EXAMPLE 16.7.** ◆

A more complex sequencing example demonstrates the possibility of multiple records with the same sequence number. Given the file ACCOUNT(ano,type,balance), the following rules create a REPORTL file that contains all the accounts with negative balances before all the others:

$$\text{ACCOUNT}(ano,type,bal),\ bal<0 \rightarrow$$
$$\text{REPORTL}(1,ano,type,bal)$$
$$\text{ACCOUNT}(ano,type,bal),\ bal\geq0 \rightarrow$$
$$\text{REPORTL}(2,ano,type,bal)$$

◆ **EXAMPLE 16.8.** ◆

Given the files ACCOUNT(ano,type,balance), and TRANSACTION(tno,ano,amount), the following rules update the account balances into a new file NACCOUNT and define a REPORT containing the account number and new balance for each account, assuming exactly one transaction per account:

REPORT(1,"account number","new balance")
ACCOUNT(ano,type,bal), TRANSACTION(tno,ano,a),
$\qquad$ nb = bal + a → NACCOUNT(ano,type,nb)
NACCOUNT(ano,type,nb) → REPORT(2,ano,nb)

Alternatively, the updating can be done recursively without creating a new NACCOUNT file in each period, but by time-stamping all records and creating an NACCOUNT(ano,type,bal,time) file. Under this strategy ACCOUNT(ano,type,balance) contains only the initial values, and a TRANSACTION(tno,ano,amount,time) contains time-stamped transactions.

ACCOUNT(ano,type,bal) → NACCOUNT(ano,type, bal,1)
NACCOUNT(ano,type,bal,t),
TRANSACTION(tno,ano,a,t) →
$\qquad$ NACCOUNT(ano, type,bal + a, t + 1)

and a REPORT6(line,ano,nb) for the time period 6 would be defined as:

REPORT6(1,"account number","new balance")
NACCOUNT(ano,type,bal,6) → REPORT6(2,ano,bal)

This example assumes exactly one transaction per account. The assumption can be expressed explicitly to ensure it is not violated by the system:

ACCOUNT(ano,type,bal) $\rightarrow$

TRANSACTION(TR(ano),ano,AM(ano))

TRANSACTION(tno,ano,bal) $\rightarrow$

ACCOUNT(ano,T(ano),B(ano))

stating that for every account there is a corresponding transaction, and vice versa. In general, there will be accounts with no corresponding transaction. To update those account records would require a negative condition checking for nonexistence of transactions corresponding to an account:

TRANSACTION(tno,ano,amount) $\rightarrow$ TRANS(ano)

ACCOUNT(ano,type,bal), $-$TRANS(ano) $\rightarrow$

NACCOUNT(ano,type,bal)

where TRANS(ano) contains all account numbers with corresponding transactions. Note that $-$TRANS(ano) is different from $-$TRANSACTION(tno,ano,amount) where the latter is satisfied many times for each ano since there are many (tno,amount) values that do not correspond to a transaction for that account. $-$TRANS(ano), on the other hand, is satisfied once for each ano, and only if no transactions exist for that account.

## Prolog

Prolog, programming in logic, is the most commonly used logic-based environment. It is more restricted than the general logic rule environment. It uses Horn clauses, rules with only one condition on the right-hand side, and it provides no standard aggregate functions such as SUM or MAXIMUM. Instead, it provides some commands corresponding to the actions of a production rule environment such as "insert" and "delete". The rest of the language is identical to the standard logic rule rotation where a rule $c_1, \ldots, c_n \to a$, is expressed as $a_1 := c_1, \ldots, c_n$. Files in prolog can be created by merely listing individual records as instances of predicates.

## QUESTIONS

1. A portfolio database contains the following files:

   - ACCOUNT(ano,type,balance) containing the account number, account type, and account balance for each account in the portfolio of a customer
   - INTEREST(type,frate,crate) containing the type of account, the expected future interest rate, and the current interest rate for that type of account

   Write logic rules to create the file **TRANSACTION** (ano,amount) where each transaction indicates a movement of funds into an account ano. A negative amount indicates a movement of funds out of the account ano. Transactions come in pairs since each movement takes equal amount of funds from one account and deposits it into another. The amount of funds transferred from account 1 to account 2 is given by the following formula:

   $$((frate2 - crate2) - (frate1 - crate1)) \times (balance1 + balance2)$$

2. Given the files ACCOUNT(ano,type,balance), TRANSACTION(ano,amount) as described in Question 1; write logic rules to print a portfolio statement containing the account number and the new balance for each account. A similar example was given in Example 16.8. The example assumes only one transaction per customer. Your rules should relax this assumption.

3. Locate a commercial logic system, such as prolog, in your computing center. Identify the differences between your system and the standard notation used in this chapter.

Load ACCOUNT and INTEREST files into your system with fictitious data.

4.  Repeat Questions 1 and 2 for your system.


# BIBLIOGRAPHY

Grant, J. *A Logical Introduction to Databases.* San Diego, CA: Academic Press, 1988.

Gray, P. *Logic, Algebra and Databases.* New York: John Wiley & Sons, 1984.

Hayes-Roth, F. *Building Expert Systems.* Reading, MA: Addison-Wesley, 1983.

Jackson, P. *Introduction to Expert Systems.* Reading, MA: Addison-Wesley, 1984.

Kowalski, R. A. *Logic for Problem Solving.* New York: North Holland, 1979.

♦

# Chapter 17

# Inference

The major advantage of logic rules is their ability to create new knowledge from existing knowledge. This ability is more general than the creation of new data from existing data, which all procedures do, but it involves creation of new rules from existing rules. Data represent the state of the system at a given time, whether they are extensional or intensional data. Rules, on the other hand, describe the behavior of the system at all times by capturing time invariant properties of data. For example, the rule stating that all accounts have positive balances is quite different from the observation that all account balances in the database are positive. The database refers to the current point in time; the rule requires the account balances to remain positive at all times. The time-invariant property of rules makes them a good candidate for use not only to create new data, but also to describe and constrain existing data. The description of the data is important to designers to ensure correctness, and the constraints are important to system administrators to maintain the correctness of the data by catching errors and exceptions. *Inference* is the logical process through which new knowledge is created from existing knowledge. Three types of inference are distinguished. *Derivation* is the creation of new data from existing data and rules, *deduction* is the creation of new rules from existing rules, and *induction* is the creation of new rules from existing data and rules.

## *Derivation*

The *derivation* of new data from existing data using rules is the basis of the distinction between extensional and intensional data. Intensional data are derived from the extensional data by using the rules. Chapter 16 has dealt with this issue. The only remaining problem is the strategies used to implement the derivations. Since intensional files may be infinitely large, their derivation should be controlled by requests. The derivation should be triggered by a request and halted as soon as the request has been met. The only controversy relates to the derivation of intermediate data and the sequence in which they are derived. Forward chaining and backward chaining are the two basic strategies, with some combination of the two usually accepted as a third possible strategy. *Forward chaining* refers to the strategy of starting with existing data and creating new data as the rules apply until the request is met. This strategy is straightforward but inefficient, since the creation of new data is random and not guided toward the requested data. *Backward chaining* starts with the requested data as a goal and identifies rules that could possibly derive those data, and sets the data needed by those rules as subgoals. The process continues until all required subgoals are met by the existing data. This strategy is complex but usually more efficient. The most efficient strategies involve a combination of the two strategies.

---

◆ EXAMPLE 17.1. ◆

Given the file ACCOUNT(ano,rate,balance) and the rule ACCOUNT(ano,rate,bal), nb = bal × rate → NACCOUNT (ano,rate,nb), a request for NACCOUNT(1128,$x$,$y$) can be met by forward chaining which requires the creation of NACCOUNT records until the one for 1128 is derived. Backward chaining starts with the request NACCOUNT (1128,$x$,$y$), determines the need for ACCOUNT (1128,$x$,$y$), sets it as the subgoal, and once it establishes it as true with appropriate $x$ and $y$ values, then it moves forward to create the NACCOUNT record. For most information systems where a small number of requests are made against a large reservoir of information, backward chaining is more efficient than forward chaining.

---

## Deduction

*Deduction* is the creation of new rules from existing rules. The new rules are implied by the existing ones in the sense that the correctness of the existing rules logically implies the correctness of the new rules. In that sense, deduction does not create completely novel rules (as induction does) but merely restructures existing rules for easier use or better insight. The creation of new rules should obviously be controlled by need to prevent a proliferation of rules, especially many versions of the same rule. The basic strategy is to create rules as they are needed, and eliminate the rules that are not utilized, resulting in a very dynamic environment. The most critical component in this environment is determining if a new rule is valid, that is, whether it is implied by the existing rules.

**EXAMPLE 17.2.**

Given the files A(ano,type), B(type,rate), and C(ano,rate) containing the types of accounts, rates corresponding to account types, and the rates applying to each account, respectively, and the following rule:

$$A(n,t),\ B(t,r) \rightarrow C(n,r) \tag{1}$$

establishing the rate applying to an account as the rate associated with its type. A simple deduction creates the following rule:

$$A(1118,1),\ B(1,0.05) \rightarrow C(1118,0.05) \tag{2}$$

which states that if account 1118 is of type 1, and type 1 pays 5 percent interest, then account 1118 pays 5 percent interest. This rule is clearly implied by Rule (1) by substituting 1118 for $n$, 1 for $t$, and 0.05 for $r$. If a rule is correct for all $(n,t,r)$ values, then it is clearly also correct for the specific values (1118,1,0.05). This principle is called the *substitution principle.* Many other rules are implied by Rule (1), by substituting different values for each variable. Moreover, not all variables have to be substituted with constants. Only some variables may be substituted with constants, and others may be left as variables, or substituted with functions. Some rules implied by Rule (1) are shown below.

$$A(n,1),\ B(1,0.05) \rightarrow C(n,0.05) \tag{3}$$

states that if type 1 pays 5 percent interest then all type 1 accounts pay 5 percent interest. It is obtained from Rule (1) by substituting 1 for $t$ and 0.05 for $r$.

$$A(n,1),\ B(1,R) \rightarrow C(n,R) \tag{4}$$

**EXAMPLE 17.2.** (*Continued*)

states that if there is an interest $R$ paid by type 1, then all type 1 accounts have that rate $R$. This rule is obtained by substituting the constant 1 for $t$, and the function R for $r$. Note that this rule is different from

$$A(n,1),\ B(1,r) \rightarrow C(n,r) \tag{5}$$

which states that any interest rate associated with type 1 is also associated with all accounts of type 1, where Rule (4) asserts the existence of only one such rate $R$. The two rules are different when there are multiple rates associated with each account type. Rule (5) associates all rates associated with type 1 with all accounts of type 1; Rule (4) associates only one of those rates with all type 1 accounts. This distinction follows from the assumption that all variables are universally quantified, but functions assert only the existence of a value. Rules (4) and (5) are both implied by Rule (1). Moreover, Rule (5) implies Rule (4) since if a rule is true for all interest rates, then there is certainly an interest rate $R$ one can find for which the rule holds.

$$A(n,T),\ B(T,R) \rightarrow C(n,R) \tag{6}$$

states that there is a (type,rate) pair $(T,R)$ such that if $R$ is associated with $T$ then all accounts of type $T$ pay the rate $R$. This rule is implied by (1) by substituting $T$ for $t$, and $R$ for $r$. On the other hand,

$$A(n,1) \rightarrow C(n,0.05) \tag{7}$$

is not implied by (1). It states that all type 1 accounts pay 5 percent interest. Clearly, this is not implied by 1, unless we also know that type 1 is associated with 5 percent interest rate. A number of rules are implied by (7).

$$A(n, 1) \rightarrow C(n, R) \qquad\qquad (8)$$

states that there is a rate $R$ associated with all type 1 accounts. This rule is implied by Rule 7. Clearly, if all type 1 accounts have the rate 5 percent, then they do have a rate $R$ in common, which happens to be 5 percent. In the reverse direction, Rule (8) does not imply Rule 7 since knowing that all type 1 accounts have a common rate $R$ says nothing about its value, whether it is 5 percent or something else.

$$A(n, 1) \rightarrow C(n, R(n)) \qquad\qquad (9)$$

states that all type 1 accounts have rates. It does not have to be the same rate for all, since $R(n)$ can have a different value for each $n$. This rule is implied by (7), since if all type 1 accounts have the rate 0.05, clearly they all have rates. Using the same argument, (8) implies this rule too, since if all type 1 accounts have a common rate R, then clearly they all have rates.

$$A(n, T(n)) \rightarrow C(n, R(n)) \qquad\qquad (10)$$

states that all accounts that have types also have rates. This rule is not implied by any of the rules so far, but it implies Rule 9. Since all accounts with types also have rates, then all type 1 accounts would also have rates.

All the implications so far have been derived by substitution. Substitution is a major tool of deduction. However, not all substitutions are correct. Only the following substitutions are allowed:

1. Constants and functions can be substituted for variables (as in Rules 2 through 6).

2. New functions can be substituted for existing functions.
3. Functions can be substituted for constants on the right-hand side (as in Rules 8 and 9).
4. Constants can be substituted for functions on the left-hand side (as in the implications of Rule 9 by Rule 10).

Unfortunately, not all deductions can be done simply by substitution.

◆ **EXAMPLE 17.3.** ◆

Given the files A(ano,type), B(type,rate), C(ano,rate), and the rule:

$$A(n,t), \ B(t,r) \rightarrow C(n,r) \qquad (1)$$

prove that there is a (type,rate) pair $(T,R)$ such that all accounts of type $T$ have the rate $R$:

$$A(n,T), \ B(t,R) \rightarrow C(n,R)$$

Note that $R$ is not required to be the rate of $T$, but some rate associated with a type $t$. This deduction can not be done by mere substitution, since substitutions must be done uniformly throughout a rule. A more general strategy is required. The strategy is to assume the left-hand side of the goal and to try to infer the right-hand side by using the given rules and substitution.

| A($n$,$T$) (2)<br>B($t$,$R$) (3) | B($T$,$R$) (4) | C($n$,$R$) (5) |
|---|---|---|
| (Assume) | (From (3) by substituting $T$ for $t$) | (From (1), (2), and (4) by substituting $T$ for $t$ and $R$ for $r$) |

Similarly, given the same files and rule, to prove that if every account has a type, and every type has a rate, then every account has a rate, we have

$$A(n,t),\ B(t,r) \rightarrow C(n,r) \tag{1}$$
$$A(n,T(n)) \tag{2}$$
$$B(t,R(t)) \tag{3}$$

to prove

$$C(n,S(n))$$

| $B(T(n),R(T(n)))$ (4) | $C(n,R(T(n)))$ (5) | $C(n,S(n))$ (6) |
|---|---|---|
| (From (3) by substituting $T(n)$ for $t$) | (From (1), (2), and (4) by substituting $T(n)$ for $t$, $R(T(n))$ for $r$) | (From (5) by substituting $S$ for $R(T)$) |

Such an intuitive strategy is effective for simple deductions. However, it is not complete. It fails to deal with negated and OR'ed conditions. A general procedure is essential for a systematic approach and possible automation of the deduction process. The *resolution algorithm* is such a general procedure, consisting of four steps.

1. Each rule $C_1, \ldots, C_n \rightarrow A_1, \ldots, A_n$ is expressed as a set of conditions $\{-C_1, \ldots, -C_n, A_1, \ldots, A_m\}$, to be interpreted as $-C_1 \vee \ldots \vee -C_n \vee A_1 \vee, \ldots \vee A_m$;

2. The rule to be derived, $C_1, \ldots, C_n \rightarrow A_1, \ldots, A_m$ is expressed as $n+m$ sets $\{C_1\}, \ldots, \{C_n\}, \{-A_1\}, \ldots, \{-A_m\}$ after the following transformations:

   a. Replace all functions with distinct variables, and all variables with distinct functions.

   b. For each function, add as arguments all variables except those that have that function as an argument.

   c. Drop all arguments of all variables.

The resulting sets are interpreted as $C_1 \wedge \ldots \wedge C_n \wedge -A_1 \wedge \ldots \wedge -A_m$ which is the negation of the goal. Now the task is to show that these conditions are inconsistent. The given rules and the negation of the goal cannot all be true, implying that the goal must be true whenever the given rules are.

3.  Given two sets of conditions $\{C_1, \ldots, C_n\}$ and $\{D_1, \ldots, D_m\}$ and $C_i = -D_j$ with appropriate substitutions, create a new rule denoted by the set $\{C_1, \ldots, C_n, D_1, \ldots, D_m\} - \{C_i, D_j\}$ with the appropriate substitutions. Variables can be substituted by constants, functions, or other variables, as long as all occurrences of a variable are substituted for uniformly.

4.  The creation of a null set of conditions indicates a successful termination of the deduction algorithm, since it proves the inconsistency of the given rules and the negation of the goal. All provable goals result in null sets; however, unprovable goals may result in a nonterminating procedure.

◆ **EXAMPLE 17.4.** ◆

Given the files A(ano,type), B(type,rate), and C(ano,rate), and the rule

$$A(n,t), \, B(t,r) \rightarrow C(n,r)$$

of Example 17.2; to prove by resolution that

$$A(n, 1), \, B(1,r) \rightarrow C(n,r)$$

the following sets are created:

$$\{-A(n,t), \ -B(t,r), \ C(n,r)\} \qquad (1)$$
$$\{A(N, 1)\} \qquad (2)$$
$$\{B(1,R)\} \qquad (3)$$
$$\{-C(N,R)\} \qquad (4)$$

Note that all variables of the goal are replaced by distinct functions as required by step 2 of the resolution algorithm.

Resolving (1) and (2) by substituting $N$ for $n$, and 1 for $t$

$$\{-B(1,r),\ C(N,r)\} \qquad (5)$$

Resolving (3) and (5) by substituting $R$ for $r$

$$\{C(N,R)\} \qquad (6)$$

Resolving (4) and (6)

$$\{\ \} \qquad \text{completes the proof.}$$

Similarly, given the same files and the rule

$$A(n,t),\ D(t,r) \rightarrow C(n,r)$$

of Example 17.2; to prove

$$A(n,T),\ B(T,R) \rightarrow C(n,R)$$

the following sets are created:

$$\{-A(n,t),\ -B(t,r),\ C(n,r)\} \qquad (1)$$
$$\{A(N(t,r),t)\} \qquad (2)$$
$$\{B(t,r)\} \qquad (3)$$
$$\{-C(N(t,r),r)\} \qquad (4)$$

Note that all variables of the goal are transformed into functions, and all functions are transformed into variables. As required by step 2 of the resolution algorithm, the functions have all the variables as arguments.

Resolving (1) and (3)

$$\{-A(n,t),\ C(n,r)\} \qquad (5)$$

**EXAMPLE 17.4.** (*Continued*)

Resolving (2), (4), and (5) by substituting $N(t,r)$ for $n$

$$\{\ \}$$

Similarly, given the same files and the rule

$$A(n,1) \rightarrow C(n,0.05)$$

to prove

$$A(n,1) \rightarrow C(n,R(n))$$

the following sets are created:

$$\{-A(n,1),\ C(n,0.05)\} \qquad (1)$$
$$\{A(N,1)\} \qquad (2)$$
$$\{-C(N,r)\} \qquad (3)$$

Note that the function $N$ in the goal sets does not have the variable $r$ as an argument. This result is achieved by following the resolution algorithm step b as follows:

$$A(n,1) \rightarrow C(n,R(N)) \qquad \text{is given.}$$

Replacing all variables with functions, and functions with variables

$$A(N,1) \rightarrow C(n,r(N))$$

Adding to each function as argument a variables except those that have that function as an argument does not change the rule. The function $N$ does not take $r$ as an argument, since $r$ has $N$ as an argument. Finally, dropping all arguments of variables

$$A(N,1) \rightarrow C(N,r)$$

Converting to set form

$$\{A(N,1)\}$$
$$\{-C(N,r)\}$$

Resolving (1) and (2) by substituting $N$ for $n$

$$\{C(n,0.05)\} \qquad\qquad (4)$$

Resolving (3) and (4) by substituting $N$ for $n$, 0.05 for $r$

$$\{\ \}$$

◆ **EXAMPLE 17.5.** ◆

Given the file A(ano,type), B(type,rate), and C(ano,rate), and the rules

$$A(a,t),\ B(t,r) \rightarrow C(a,r)$$
$$C(a,r) \rightarrow A(a,T(a,r))$$
$$C(a,r) \rightarrow B(T(a,r),r)$$

which define C in terms of A and B and no other records.
   The goal is to prove that if there is exactly one type for each account, and there is exactly one rate for each type, then there is exactly one rate for each account. In other words, if A is single-valued from ano to type, and B is single-valued from type to rate, then C is single-valued from ano to rate. Expressing it in rules, if

$$A(n,t_1),\ A(n,t_2) \rightarrow t_1 = t_2 \qquad \text{and}$$
$$B(t,r_1),\ B(t,r_2) \rightarrow r_1 = r_2 \qquad \text{then}$$
$$C(n,r_1),\ C(n,r_2) \rightarrow r_1 = r_2$$

**EXAMPLE 17.5.** (*Continued*)

Converting all rules and the goal into sets of conditions

$$\{-A(n,t),\ -B(t,r),\ C(n,r)\} \tag{1}$$
$$\{-C(n,r),\ A(n,T(n,r))\} \tag{2}$$
$$\{-C(n,r),\ B(T(n,r),r)\} \tag{3}$$
$$\{-A(n_1 t_1),\ -A(n_1 t_2),\ t_1=t_2\} \tag{4}$$
$$\{-B(t_1 r_1),\ -B(t_1 r_2),\ r_1=r_2\} \tag{5}$$
$$\{C(N,R_1)\} \tag{6}$$
$$\{C(N,R_2)\} \tag{7}$$
$$\{R_1\neq R_2\} \tag{8}$$

Resolving (2) and (6) by substituting $N$ for $n$, and $R_1$ for $r$

$$\{A(N,T(N,R_1))\} \tag{9}$$

Resolving (2) and (7) by substituting $R_2$ for r

$$\{A(N,T(N,R_2))\} \tag{10}$$

Resolving (3) and (6) by substituting $N$ for $n$ and $R_1$ for $r$

$$\{B(T(N,R_1),R_1)\} \tag{11}$$

Resolving (3) and (7) by substituting $N$ for $n$ and $R_2$ for $r$

$$\{B(T(N,R_2),R_2)\} \tag{12}$$

Resolving (4), (9), and (10) by substituting $N$ for $n$, $T(N,R_1)$ for $t_1$, and $T(N,R_2)$ for $t_2$

$$\{T(N,R_1)=T(N,R_2)\} \tag{13}$$

By substituting $T(N,R_1)$ for $T(N,R_2)$ in (12)

$$\{B(T(N,R_1),R_2)\} \tag{14}$$

Resolving (5), (11), and (14) by substituting $T(N,R_1)$ for $t$

$$\{R_1 = R_2\} \tag{15}$$

Resolving (8) and (15)

$$\{\ \} $$

◆ EXAMPLE 17.6. ◆

Given the files A(ano,type), B(type,rate), and C(ano,rate) and the rules

$$A(n,t),\ B(t,r) \rightarrow C(n,r)$$
$$C(n,r) \rightarrow A(n,T(n,r))$$
$$C(n,r) \rightarrow B(T(n,r),r)$$

If A and B are injective, then prove that C is also injective. A relation A(ano,type) is injective from ano to type if ano have no types in common, although they can each have multiple types. In other words, if

$$A(n_1,t_1),\ A(n_2,t_2),\ n_1 \neq n_2 \rightarrow t_1 \neq t_2 \qquad \text{and}$$
$$B(t_1,r_1),\ B(t_2,r_2),\ t_1 \neq t_2 \rightarrow r_1 \neq r_2$$

Prove that

$$C(n_1,r_1),\ C(n_2,r_2),\ n_1 \neq n_2 \rightarrow r_1 \neq r_2$$

Converting all rules into sets

$$\{-A(n,t),\ -B(t,r),\ C(n,r)\} \tag{1}$$
$$\{-C(n,r),\ A(n,T(n,r))\} \tag{2}$$
$$\{-C(n,r),\ B(T(n,r),r)\} \tag{3}$$
$$\{-A(n_1,t_1),\ -A(n_2,t_2),\ n_1 = n_2,\ t_1 \neq t_2\} \tag{4}$$
$$\{-B(t_1,r_1),\ -B(t_2,r_2),\ t_1 = t_2,\ r_1 \neq r_2\} \tag{5}$$
$$\{C(N_1,R_1)\} \tag{6}$$
$$\{C(N_2,R_2)\} \tag{7}$$
$$\{N_1 \neq N_2\} \tag{8}$$
$$\{R_1 = R_2\} \tag{9}$$

**EXAMPLE 17.6.** (*Continued*)

Resolving (2) and (6) by substituting $R_1$ for $r$, $N_1$ for $n$

$$\{A(N_1,T(N_1,R_1))\} \qquad (10)$$

Resolving (2) and (7) by substituting $R_2$ for $r$, $N_2$ for $n$

$$\{A(N_2,T(N_2,R_2))\} \qquad (11)$$

Resolving (4), (8), (10), and (11) by substituting $T(N_1,R_1)$ for $t_1$ and $T(N_2,R_2)$ for $t_2$

$$\{T(N_1,R_1)\neq T(N_2,R_2)\} \qquad (12)$$

Resolving (3) and (6) by substituting $R_1$ for $r$, $N_1$ for $n$

$$\{B(T(N_1,R_1),N_1)\} \qquad (13)$$

Resolving (3) and (7) by substituting $R_2$ for $r$, $N_2$ for $n$

$$\{B(T(N_2,R_2),R_2)\} \qquad (14)$$

Resolving (5), (12), (13), (14) by substituting $T(N_1,R_1)$ for $t_1$ and $T(N_2,R_2)$ for $t_2$

$$\{R_1\neq R_2\} \qquad (15)$$

Resolving (9) and (15)

$$\{\ \}$$

◆ **EXAMPLE 17.7.** ◆

Given the same files and rules as above, if A is single valued, and B is injective, then C is semi-single-valued. A file C(ano,rate) is said to be semi-single-valued from ano to rate if ano either have no rates in common or they have exactly the same rates. In logic rule notation, if

$$A(n,t_1), A(n,t_2) \rightarrow t_1 = t_2 \quad \text{and}$$
$$B(t_1,r_1), B(t_2,r_2), t_1 \neq t_2 \rightarrow r_1 \neq r_2 \quad \text{then}$$
$$C(n_1,r_1), C(n_1,r_2), C(n_2,r_1) \rightarrow C(n_2,r_2)$$

Converting all rules to set notation

$$\{-A(n,t), -B(t,r), C(n,r)\} \tag{1}$$
$$\{-C(n,r), A(n,T(n,r))\} \tag{2}$$
$$\{-C(n,r), B(T(n,r),r)\} \tag{3}$$
$$\{-A(n,t_1), -A(n,t_2), t_1 = t_2\} \tag{4}$$
$$\{-B(t_1,r_1), -B(t_2,r_2), t_1 = t_2, r_1 \neq r_2\} \tag{5}$$
$$\{C(N_1,R_1\} \tag{6}$$
$$\{C(N_1,R_2)\} \tag{7}$$
$$\{C(N_2,R_1)\} \tag{8}$$
$$\{-C(N_2,R_2)\} \tag{9}$$

Resolving (2) and (6) by substitution $N_1$ for $n$, $R_1$ for $r$

$$\{A(N_1,T(N_1,R_1)\} \tag{10}$$

Resolving (2) and (7)

$$\{A(N_1,T(N_1,R_2)\} \tag{11}$$

Resolving (2) and (8)

$$\{A(N_2,T(N_2,R_1)\} \tag{12}$$

Resolving (3) and (6)

$$\{B(T(N_1,R_1), R_1)\} \tag{13}$$

Resolving (3) and (7)

$$\{B(T(N_1,R_2),R_2)\} \tag{14}$$

**EXAMPLE 17.7.** (*Continued*)

Resolving (3) and (8)

$$\{B(T(N_2,R_1),R_1)\} \tag{15}$$

Resolving (4), (10), and (11)

$$T(N_1,R_1) = T(N_1,R_2) \tag{16}$$

Resolving (5), (13), and (15)

$$T(N_1,R_1) = T(N_2,R_1) \tag{17}$$

Substituting in (16) from (17)

$$T(N_1,R_2) = T(N_2,R_1) \tag{18}$$

Substituting in (12) from (18)

$$\{A(N_2, T(N_1,R_2))\} \tag{19}$$

Resolving (1), (14), and (19)

$$\{C(N_2,R_2)\} \tag{20}$$

Resolving (9) and (20)

$$\{ \; \} $$

## Induction

*Induction* is the process by which new rules are created from existing data and rules. Unlike deduction, induction does not produce rules whose correctness is implied by the existing knowledge, but the rules it creates are hypotheses that may or may not be correct. These rules have to be constantly tested against the data, and their reliability has to be modified according to how they hold up against evidence in time. Each such rule has a "confidence factor" attached to it, which indicates how well the rule stood up when scrutinized against data over time. Initially, a new rule has a very low confidence factor, and in time as it is checked against data, its confidence factor goes up or down depending on the positive or negative confirmation it receives. The rules with a very low confidence factor below a minimum threshold are discarded, and in case of conflict between two rules, the one with a higher confidence factor is expected to dominate.

There are two general types of induction. *Analogy* is used to create rules from data. Given a file F, if there is predicate G satisfied by all records in F, then the rule F → G is hypothesized. In time, if the file F continues to support the rule F → G, it is accepted with reasonable confidence and used to make predictions about future data. Analogy is used most commonly to fill in missing data. For example, if all type 1 records in the ACCOUNT file have negative balances, then the hypothesis ACCOUNT(ano,1,bal) → bal<0 will be asserted. If the rule gains credibility in time (possibly because type 1 accounts are loans and they ordinarily have negative balances), then it will be used to predict that all type 1 accounts will have negative balances. This rule will catch accounts with positive balances, and single them out as possible violations of the system integrity. Conversely, if all negative balances belong to type 1 accounts, then the rule ACCOUNT(ano,type,bal), bal<0 → type = 1 is asserted. If the rule gains credibility in time through the support of data, then it can be used to predict missing data values, or catch errors. An account record with negative balance and missing type would be predicted as type 1. The prediction would not be absolute, but it would have confidence factor proportional to the confidence factors used in making the prediction.

The second type of induction, called *abduction*, is used to create new rules from existing rules and data. Given a rule

$C_1, \ldots, C_n \rightarrow A_1, \ldots, A_m$, the following rules are hypothesized if they are supported by the existing data:

$$C_1, \ldots, C_{i-1}, C_{i+1}, \ldots, C_n, A_j \rightarrow C_i$$

for every $i \epsilon \{1, \ldots, n\}$ and for every $j \epsilon \{1, \ldots, m\}$. If any of these rules gains credibility in time through the support of data, then they can be used to make predictions and to maintain the integrity of data. For example, given the rule

$$\text{ACCOUNT(ano,type,bal), bal} < 0 \rightarrow \text{type} = 1$$

then by abduction the following rule is hypothesized:

$$\text{ACCOUNT(ano,type,bal), type} = 1 \rightarrow \text{bal} < 0$$

Clearly, the new rule is not implied by the existing rule. It is only a reasonable hypothesis, and even then only if it is supported by existing data. In time, if it continues to be supported by data, it will become a usable rule.

## QUESTIONS

1. Given the files A(ano,type), B(type,rate), C(ano,rate), and the rules

$$A(n,t), B(t,r) \rightarrow C(n,r)$$
$$C(n,r) \rightarrow A(n,T(n,r))$$
$$C(n,r) \rightarrow B(T(n,r),r)$$

prove that if A is single-valued from ano to type, and B is injective from type to rate, then C is semi-single-valued from ano to rate.

2. Given the same rules, list all the rules you can hypothesize by abduction.

# BIBLIOGRAPHY

Chang, C. L., Lee, R. C. T. *Symbolic Logic and Mechanical Theorem Proving.* San Diego, CA: Academic Press, 1973.

Grant, J. *A Logical Introduction to Databases.* San Diego, CA: Academic Press, 1988.

Holland, J. H., Holyoak, K. F., Nisbett, R. F., Thagard, P. R. *Induction: Process of Inference, Learning, and Discovery.* Cambridge, MA: The MIT Press, 1986.

Jacobs, B. E. *Applied Database Logic.* Englewood Cliffs, NJ: Prentice Hall, 1985.

Kowalski, R. A. *Logic for Problem Solving.* New York: North Holland, 1979.

Robinson, J. A. *Logic: Form and Function.* New York: North Holland, 1979.

*Chapter 18*

◆

# Knowledge Base Management

Organizational knowledge base application systems can contain large numbers of rules, and the management of these knowledge bases is an emerging discipline of study. There are a variety of issues such as the storage and retrieval of rules, combining of rules to build applications and their execution, maintaining consistency and completeness of the system, management of fuzzy information and nondeterminism, knowledge acquisition, and development strategies.

## Storage and Retrieval

Rules have to be stored as data and retrieved as needed to respond to requests. With large numbers of rules in the system, efficiency of storage and retrieval mechanisms is critical. Since, unlike programs, rules do not call each other, but they are executed as they become relevant, all rules potentially have to be checked against the database at all times to determine their relevance. Clearly, sequential checking of rules for each goal is an unacceptable strategy. Rules have to be indexed with respect to relevant attributes and clustered for efficient retrieval. For example, to insert a new account record into the files of a bank, all rules describing account records must be located, retrieved, and executed against the new record to insure the new record does not violate any of the rules. Similarly, to update the account files, all rules that create new account records should be located for completeness. The storage and retrieval of rules are pure database problems by viewing rules as text data. However, effective indexing of rules requires an understanding of rules as executable statements, and an effective identification of its components for indexing.

## Completeness and Consistency

Once the rules are stored for effective retrieval, execution is controlled by goals. Every goal triggers a search for relevant rules, and the retrieval of all those for execution. Completeness requires that all relevant rules be identified and retrieved; consistency requires that conflicting rules be reconciled. One approach to consistency is to eliminate all rules that conflict with the more established rules. This approach eliminates all inconsistency from the system, but it is unrealistic with larger systems. In large systems, inconsistent rules are allowed to reside in the system in the hope that one of the rules creating the conflict will drop out in time as the evidence accumulates. Meanwhile, the conflicts are resolved for each goal individually, by assigning greater weight to the more established rules with greater confidence factors. Using either strategy, it is critical that all new data and rules are tested against the existing rules, and all inconsistencies are brought to the attention of the rule base manager. The entry into the system should be controlled diligently in larger shared systems to maintain the integrity and the reliability of the system.

## Fuzzy Information

Knowledge bases are able to deal with information even if it is not complete, consistent, and reliable. Hypotheses, speculations, hunches, claims, classifications, and subjective descriptions contain a lot of information when they are accumulated. Even the lack of information is often meaningful to a careful observer. The information that is not definitive is called fuzzy. Both data and rules may be fuzzy. Two types of fuzziness can occur. One type is caused by lack of information, the other by the existence of nondefinite information.

Lack of information may be due to missing data, rules, or both. Missing data values are called *null values*. The database contains a special symbol to indicate null values. For example, if the account type of an account is not known, the special null value is entered into that field in the database. However, the null value can not be treated like other values in the database, since it has a special meaning. Retrieving the accounts whose types are unknown would cause no problems, but retrieving all accounts with a type other than 1 would return all accounts with null types since null value is different from 1. In all likelihood, some of the unknown types may actually be 1, hence producing a misleading answer to the query. Clearly, a distinction between accounts known to be not type 1, and those not known to be type 1 should be distinguished. The problem is exacerbated with the addition of rules into the system. If there is no rule implying the type of an account as 1, clearly we cannot assume that the type is not 1, but only when there is a rule that implies that the type is not 1. Moreover, if there is a rule that implies the type of an account is either 1 or 2, that information is useful when we need a list of accounts containing types 1 and 2. That list would have to contain not only the accounts known to be type 1 and the accounts known to be type 2, but also the accounts known to be type 1 or type 2. For a complete treatment of unknown information, a three-valued logic is necessary, containing not only TRUE or FALSE but also UNKNOWN as a primitive value.

Nondefinite information is equally difficult to deal with. If there is some evidence that an account may be of type 1, that information can be captured as fuzzy data with some confidence factor attached to it. Clearly, response to queries now would have to contain the confidence factors. Type of an account may be returned as 1 with 60 percent confidence, and 2 with 15 percent confidence. Rules can also have confidence factors attached to them, especially if they are hypotheses created by induction as discussed in Chapter 17. As new data and new rules are derived, their confidence factors have to be computed from the existing confidence factors. For example, if the type of an account is known to be 1 with 60 percent confidence, and a rule with 20 percent confidence implies that its type is 1 with 80 percent confidence, then what is the final confidence we have in this fact? A fuzzy logic to combine confidence factors over logical operators has been developed, but it is beyond the scope of this book.

## Development

A real-life knowledge base application system may contain a large number of rules in addition to a large database. Acquisition of all this information is a difficult task. Especially difficult to acquire are the rules, since they reflect the expertise of a variety of users, and they are usually entered into the system independent of each other over a long period of time. Who enters the rules, under what conditions, who checks the correctness and consistency of rules, how the inconsistencies are resolved, what limits are placed on the growth of the system, and who decides what is relevant to a large organizational system are all difficult questions faced by knowledge base managers. Development of a knowledge base application is usually a long and tedious process involving large numbers of people over a long period of time. Unlike other types of applications, though, the involvement of those providing information into a knowledge base application is much less than full time and is often minimal. A large number of experts in a variety of fields provide their expertise and insight to an organizational system. Most of these experts have minimal understanding of system development issues, and their commitment to the final product is also minimal. Moreover, they all work independently, and their contributions to the system are intermittent and disconnected. The responsibility is on knowledge base management systems and the system manager to coordinate all these independent efforts and to insure the stable and consistent growth of the system as the contributions come in. This type of development is usually referred to as "evolutionary development," since the system is not developed from an overall design but evolves over time from bits and pieces of information gathered.

## *Examples*

Because of the effort and time that is necessary to develop knowledge base applications, some individual applications are as well known as the tools used to develop them. There are many knowledge base applications in use today. They are used mostly as decision support systems, to aid and advise decision makers in a variety of professions. Among the most widely known examples are **MYCIN**, used to aid physicians in diagnosing infectious diseases; **PROSPECTOR**, used to aid geologists in mineral explorations; R1, used to aid computer engineers in configuring hardware systems; **ROSIE**, in advising lawyers in legal analysis; **ELIZA**, helping psychologists in nondirective psychotherapy; **DENDRAL**, used in chemical analysis of organic compounds, and a number of smaller applications in accounting, auditing, tax law, financial investments analysis, insurance claims adjustment, new product design, consumer issues, and law enforcement.

Knowledge base systems are also used to accept and interpret natural language. The following excerpts from the interaction of users with three knowledge base applications provide a good sample of how far these systems have come and the potential they hold.

---

◆ **EXAMPLE 18.1.** ◆

The following is an excerpt from a dialog between a user and the application system GUS which simulates the behavior of a travel agent:

GUS: Hello. My name is GUS. I can help you plan a simple trip by air. Where do you want to go?

USER: I want to go to San Diego on May 28.

GUS: What time do you want to leave?

USER: I must be in San Diego before 10 am.

GUS: Would you like PSA flight 102 that arrives at 9:15 am?

USER: What is the next flight?

GUS: Air California flight 310 that leaves at 8:30 am and arrives at 10:00 am.

USER: I'll take the first one.

GUS: In what name should I make a reservation, please?

USER: Dan Bobrow.

GUS: I have confirmed the following flight: PSA flight 102 on Wednesday May 28 from San Jose to San Diego that leaves at 7:30 am and arrives at 9:15 am. What date do you want to return on?

USER: On Friday, in the evening.

GUS: Would you like the flight that leaves at 7:45 pm?

USER: That's fine.

**EXAMPLE 18.1.** (*Continued*)

GUS: I have confirmed the following flight: PSA flight 307 on Friday May 30 from San Diego to San Jose that leaves at 7:45 pm and arrives at 9:30 pm. Thank you for calling. Goodbye.

◆ **EXAMPLE 18.2.** ◆

The following is an excerpt from a dialog between a user and the application system MYCIN that diagnoses infectious diseases:

MYCIN: Please give the date and the approximate time when signs or symptoms of the primary bacteremia first appeared.
USER: May.5
MYCIN: From what site was the specimen taken?
USER: Blood.
MYCIN: When was this blood culture taken?
USER: May.9
MYCIN: Is organism a rod or coccus?
USER: Rod.
MYCIN: The gram stain of the organism?
USER: Gramneg.
MYCIN: Have there been positive cultures from sites not associated with this infection?
USER: No.
MYCIN: Did organism grow aerobically?
USER: Yes.
MYCIN: Did organism grow anaerobically?
USER: Yes.
MYCIN: What is the suspected portal for entry of organism into this sterile site?
USER: Gastrointestinal tract.
MYCIN: My therapy recommendation will be based on

the following probable infections and potential causative organisms:

1. The organism may be PSEUDOMONAS-AERUGINOSA.
2. The organism may be KLEBSIELLA-PNEUMONIAE.
3. The organism may be E-COLI.
4. The organism may be BACTEROIDES-FRAGILIS.
5. The organism may be ENTEROBACTER.
6. The organism may be PROTEUS-NON-MIRABILIS.

Does the patient have a clinically significant allergic reaction to any antimicrobial agent?

USER: No.
MYCIN: Patient's weight?
USER: 160 lb.
MYCIN: My preferred therapy recommendation is as follows:
In order to cover items 1, 2, 3, 5, 6:
Give:         GENTAMICIN
Dose:         119 mg q8h IV (or IM) for 10 days.
Comments: Modify dose in renal failure.

In order to cover for item 4:
Give:         CLINDAMYCIN
Dose:         595 mg. q6h IV (or IM) for 14 days.
Comments: If diarrhea or other GI symptoms develop, patient should be evaluated for possible pseudomembranous colitis.
Do you wish to see the next-choice therapy?

---

♦ **EXAMPLE 18.3.** ♦

The following is an excerpt from a dialog between a user and the application ELIZA, performing nondirective psychotherapy:

PATIENT: Men are all alike.
   ELIZA: In what way?
PATIENT: They are always bugging us about something or other.
   ELIZA: Can you think of a specific example?
PATIENT: Well, my boyfriend made me come here.
   ELIZA: Your boyfriend made you come here?
PATIENT: He says I am depressed.
   ELIZA: I am sorry to hear you are depressed.
PATIENT: It is true I am unhappy.
   ELIZA: Do you think that coming here will help you to not be unhappy?

---

♦ **EXAMPLE 18.4.** ♦

The following is an excerpt from a dialog between two knowledge base applications with no human interference. The application ELIZA, as a psychologist, and the application PARRY, as a paranoid schizophrenic, provide a good example of how the conversation deteriorates without some human input.

PARRY: I don't understand your motives.
 ELIZA: Why don't you understand my motives?
PARRY: Shouldn't I be?
 ELIZA: Why do you say that just now?
PARRY: That is just the way it is.
 ELIZA: Suppose that is just the way it were not.
PARRY: So?

> ELIZA: I am not sure I understand you fully.
> PARRY: You harp on the same questions too much.
> ELIZA: What does that similarity suggest to you?
> PARRY: I don't get you.
> ELIZA: Do you wish that you did get I?
> PARRY: It is about time you showed some interest in my feelings.
> ELIZA: Oh? I showed some interest in your feelings?

# QUESTIONS

1. Given a knowledge base with missing information, devise some questions that lead to misleading answers.

2. Develop a three-valued logic. Determine what values should be returned when one of the arguments is NULL to logical operators, AND, OR, IMPLICATION, THERE EXISTS, and FOR EVERY.

3. Locate a problem in your organization that would be appropriate as a knowledge base application. Try to decide what tools you would use to develop this application. Argue for your choice of tools.

4. Repeat Question 3 for a data processing, and a database application. In each case, argue why the problem falls into that particular area, and how you would choose a particular development tool in that area.

# BIBLIOGRAPHY

Charniak, E., McDermott, D. *Artificial Intelligence.* Reading, MA: Addison-Wesley, 1985.

Hofstadter, D. R. *Godel, Escher, Bach: An Eternal Golden Braid.* New York: Random House, 1979.

Mockler, R. J. *Knowledge Based Systems for Management Decisions.* Englewood Cliffs, NJ: Prentice-Hall, 1989.

Negoita, C. V. *Expert Systems and Fuzzy Systems.* Menlo Park, CA: Benjamin-Cummings, 1985.

Orman, L. *Evolutionary Development of Information Systems. Journal of MIS,* 1989; S(3):19–32.

Weizenbaum, J. *Computer Power and Human Reason.* New York: WH Freeman & Co., 1976.

# Index